In Search of History

Early Times – 1066

J.F. Aylett

Edward Arnold

A division of Hodder & Stoughton

LONDON   NEW YORK   MELBOURNE   AUCKLAND

© J.F. Aylett 1985

First published in Great Britain in 1985 by
Edward Arnold (Publishers) Ltd,
41 Bedford Square, London WC1B 3DQ

Edward Arnold (Australia) Pty Ltd,
80 Waverley Road, Caulfield East,
Victoria 3145, Australia

Seventh Impression 1991

British Library Cataloguing in Publication Data

Aylett, J.F.
    Early times – 1066.—(In search of history)
    1. Great Britain—History—To 1066
    I. Title   II. Series
    942.01   DA135

    ISBN 0 7131 0684 0

Illustrations by Philip Page

For Katharine

Acknowledgements

The author wishes to thank the Department of Medieval and
Later Antiquities of the British Museum for information
about the Sutton Hoo ship burial.

The Publishers wish to thank the following for their
permission to use copyright illustrations:

Crown Copyright, Dept of Environment: pp 29t & b, 77;
Crown Copyright, Scottish Development Dept: p 91;
British Library: pp 5, 67l, 75;
Novosti Press Agency: 71;
Cambridge University Collection of Aerial Photographs: pp
    7r, 20;
BBC Hulton Picture Library: pp 8, 79b;
British Museum: 9r, 13t &c, 68t, 70l, c & r, 72, 90;
Eric Kay: p 11;
Butser Ancient Farm Project Trust: p 12;
Colchester & Essex Museum: p 13b;
BBC Enterprises: pp 14, 15t & b;
Mansell Collection: pp 16, 37, 40, 45l, 48, 55(British
    Museum), 68b(British Museum), 82t, 94r;
Society of Antiquaries of London: p 21;
Ann Ronan Picture Library: p 24;
David Simson (DAS): p 25;
A F Kersting: pp 35, 46, 65r, 76, 78;
Reading Museum & Art Gallery: p 39;
Museum of London: p 43;
Rockbourne Roman Villa & Museum: p 45r;
Eric Lessing-Magnum/John Hillelson Agency Ltd: p 49;
National Monuments Record: pp 51, 92r;
Michael Holford: p 59;
Janet & Colin Bord: 60;
Bord Failte (Irish Tourist Board): p 65l;
E C Wharton-Tigar: p 66;
From a codex at Engleberg Abbey, Switzerland: 67r, 94l;
Ashmolean Museum: p 79t;
Bodleian Library: pp 82b, 83;
David Chadwick: p 86;
Ronald Sheridan's Photo Library: 87;
Diana Lanham: p 92l.

Text set in 12 on 13 point Linoterm Plantin
by The Castlefield Press, Moulton, Northampton
Printed and bound in Great Britain at The Bath Press, Avon

Contents 942.01 /943.

	Introduction	4
1	Getting to Know Early Times	6
2	The First People in Britain	8
3	Stonehenge and its Mysteries	10
4	People Begin Using Iron	12
5	Living in 'the Iron Age'	14
6	'Rome Shall be the Capital of the World'	16
7	The Romans Arrive in Britain	18
8	Attacking a Hill Fort	20
9	The Roman Army	22
10	The Druids	24
11	A Queen Called Boudica	26
12	Keeping Out the Picts	28
13	The Romans Build Roads	30
14	The Romans Build Towns	32
	Revision	35
15	Out Shopping . . .	36
16	. . . and Back at Home	38
17	A Slave's Life	40
18	Going to School	42
19	Keeping People Healthy	44
20	Bath	46
21	Roman Amusements	48
22	Roman Gods and Christianity	50
23	The Romans Leave . . .	52
24	. . . and the Anglo-Saxons Arrive	54
25	Saxon Villages	56
26	King Arthur: Is it History or Just a Story?	58
	Revision	61
27	A Saxon Hero – *Beowulf*	62
28	Saxons and the Christian Religion	64
29	Buried Treasure at Sutton Hoo	68
30	Scenes from Married Life	72
31	Crime and Punishment	74
32	The Vikings are Coming!	76
33	A King and a Legend – Alfred the Great	78
34	Reading and Writing	82
35	Sports and Pastimes	84
36	The Battle of Maldon	86
37	The Last Years of Saxon England	88
38	Looking Back	90
	Revision	93
	Writers and Sources	94
	Word List (Glossary)	95
	Index	96

Introduction

Today, I am writing this book. How do I know? Because I am here. I am doing it.

Last year, my daughter started going to school. How do I know? Because I was there when she set off. I remember it.

In 1939, the Second World War started. How do I know? Because one of my uncles fought in it. He was there. And he has told me about it.

In 55 BC, Julius Caesar came to Britain. How do I know? I wasn't there. I can't remember it. I certainly have never met anyone who was there. It was too long ago. So, how do I know?

I expect I read about it in a book. But how did the writer know? He probably wasn't there either.

The writer must have had a reason for writing it. He must have had some *evidence* to make him believe it. How do people know what happened in 55 BC?

This is how we know:
Some people wrote about it at the time.

Some people told their friends . . . and they told their friends . . . and, later on, somebody wrote about it.

Some people made pictures of it.

And some people left behind things which were found years later.

So we ought to know what happened. The trouble is that people do not always agree about what happened. Look at the picture on page 5.

It is a picture of King Arthur fighting a battle. Perhaps you have read stories about King Arthur and his Knights of the Round Table. And here you have a picture of him in action. But do you?

This picture was painted in the 14th century. But, if Arthur lived at all, he lived in the 6th century. How could someone know what he looked like 800 years later? Of course, he couldn't.

Anyway, that is not the end of the problem. Why did we write '*if* Arthur lived at all'? Surely, everyone has heard of him? He must have lived!

However, it is not as easy as that. Some historians really think that he didn't exist. Others think that he was called something else. Most of them agree that he was not a king.

History is full of problems like this. You will find some of them in this book. The book is divided into chapters. There is a full list of them on page 3.

Most chapters start with a word box like the one below.

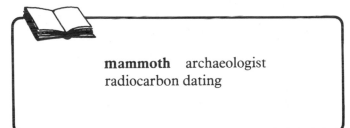

mammoth   archaeologist
radiocarbon dating

This is the word box from chapter one. It contains four special words which are used in that chapter. The words in heavy black type **like this** are explained on page 95 in the glossary. The glossary is a list of words with their meanings. If you don't understand one of these words, look it up at once.

The words in the box which are not in heavy type are made clear in the chapter itself. Do not try to look them up. They are not in the glossary.

Right after the word box comes the chapter itself. Read this part through and make sure you understand it.

At the end of most chapters is a section of evidence. Each section of evidence has a picture at the top so you can spot it quickly. This is the picture:

The evidence might be pictures or pieces of writing, or both. Sometimes the pieces of evidence may not agree with each other. You may be asked to puzzle it out for yourself.

There are questions to help you do this. You can spot the questions easily, too. They have a picture like this at the top:

Do not expect to find all the answers in the chapter or the evidence. Some questions include the words, 'What do you think . . .?' This means you will have to work out the answer for yourself. When you have made your mind up, don't be afraid to write down what *you* think. And remember to write down the reasons for your view.

Your friends may not agree with you. But even writers don't always agree. Think about King Arthur. Writers can't even agree about whether he existed! It is even more difficult to get at the truth when we go back in time about 300 000 years.

And 300 000 years ago is where this book starts . . .

1 Getting to Know Early Times

mammoth archaeologist
radiocarbon dating

History is a story. It is the story of people who lived before us and of the things they did and made. It is a story which began in Britain about 300 000 years ago. At that time, Britain was not an island. It was still joined to the mainland of Europe.

It is very hard for us to think of people living all that time ago. Even adults find it difficult to imagine such a long time ago. Perhaps the diagram below will help.

Each dot stands for 1000 years. The last dot stands for the years 1000 to 2000. It is the time when we are living. It also covers a huge range of other events: the First and Second World Wars, Guy Fawkes and even the Battle of Hastings would all come inside that one dot.

The dot beside it covers the time from Jesus Christ's birth up to 1000. Somewhere in those 1000 years, the Romans, Saxons and Vikings all came to Britain. Most of this book is about that period.

But look at the other 298 dots. They cover the other 298 000 years. All the rest of Britain's history is in there. Yet this book covers all that time in just eight or nine pages. Why do we cover all that time so quickly?

One reason is because we do not know as much about the people who lived then as we do about, for instance, the Romans. All we have left of the very earliest people are just a few stone tools. Even some later people could not write so we have to learn about them from the things they left behind.

There is another problem. New objects are still being found and we are still learning about these people and their lives. So historians sometimes have to change their ideas about how early people lived.

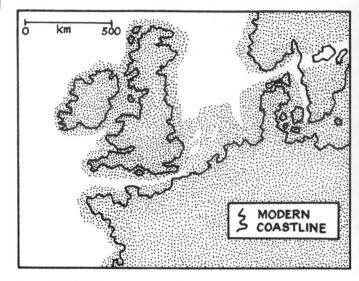

Around 300 000 years ago, Britain was still joined to the rest of Europe.

We have to rely mainly on archaeologists for our knowledge of early people. An archaeologist is a person who finds and studies old remains, such as bones or pottery.

He will have a rough idea of how old these are from the place where he finds them. However, in recent years, a more accurate method has been invented for working out how old something is.

Scientists call it radiocarbon dating. The method can be used on anything which was once alive, such as shells or bones. It measures the amount of radioactive carbon it contains.

. . . .
. . . .
. . . .
. . . .
. . . . ⊙ YOU ARE HERE!

A This is a baby **mammoth**, dug up by Russians in 1977. It died 10 000 years ago and was preserved in ice. It was so fresh that it could have been eaten.

B On the right: photographs from the air are another way of learning about the past because they can show us things which cannot be spotted on the ground. This aerial photograph shows where a farm was long ago.

In America there are some pine trees which are up to 5000 years old. Their exact age can be worked out by counting the rings in the trunks. When each ring is carbon dated, scientists can compare carbon dates with 'real' dates.

This method means that we now have a fairly good idea of how old something is. This can tell us a great deal about what people were able to do and how they lived long ago.

1 Find out which person in your group has the oldest relative. You will probably find someone has a relative who is nearly 100 years old.
2 Now, get some freize paper and some felt-tip pens. Your group is going to draw 3000 dots! Each dot will stand for 100 years of time. (If there are 30 of you, you simply draw 100 dots each.)

When you have finished, each dot will stand for 100 years of human life in this country. Put a ring round the last dot of all. This dot stands for the oldest relative you have found.
3 Explain in your own words how radiocarbon dating is used to work out how old things are.
4 a) Copy the map on page 6.
b) Mark where you live on the map. (Use an atlas if you're not sure!)
5 Make an outline sketch of the baby mammoth. Which modern animal is it like?

2 The First People in Britain

The very first people to come to Britain lived by hunting. Historians call this period the Stone Age because stone was the best material which people then had.

They learned to make weapons of wood and stone, such as spears, and bows and arrows. They also had hand-axes which they used to kill and skin animals or dig up roots. For fishing, they used harpoons and hooks made of bone.

The last part of this period is known as the New Stone Age. It began around 4000 BC when a new group of people arrived in Britain. They were the first farmers and they brought sheep, goats and cattle with them; in their boats they also had corn to sow for growing crops.

One of their first jobs was to clear some trees so they could plant these crops and graze their animals. They still had only stone axes so they chose to live on the hills where the trees were not so big. Here, they built small wooden huts with thatched roofs, held up by a circle of posts.

The New Stone Age marked a major step in human progress. For the first time, people were settling down in one place and making villages. Even more important, people were at last beginning to control their surroundings. They were shaping the land to their needs – and people have gone on doing so ever since.

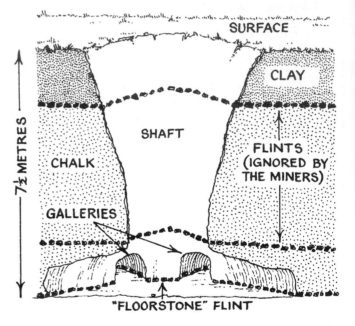

Above: a cross-section of a mine at Grime's Graves. (The mines were called this because people at first thought they were burial places.) Below: map showing places named in this chapter.

New Stone Age people probably looked like this. People could weave cloth and were sewing with bone needles.

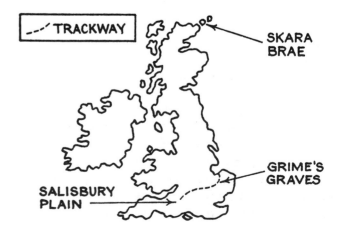

A One of seven New Stone Age houses at Skara Brae in Orkney. The village is thought to date from 2000 BC. Each house is shaped like a beehive, with stone walls, and probably had a roof made of animal skins or peat. The biggest is about 6 metres square.

B The figure of a pregnant goddess was found at Grime's Graves.

From those thousands of years ago, these people have left behind many reminders of their lives and work. One example is the **flint** mines where men dug out flint to make stone axes. People discovered that the best flint was buried well underground. So, they dug mines to get at it.

The most famous flint mines are Grime's Graves in Norfolk where over 350 mines were dug. Men hacked out the flint using picks made of deer's antlers.

Some flint was used to make axes on the spot but a lot of it must have been traded with people outside the area. Grime's Graves were close to one of the main trackways of the time. It ran across the country from the east to the south, down to Salisbury Plain, where the people of those times have left us an even greater **monument**.

1 Copy out and complete this paragraph:
Stone Age people used stone to make _____. It was the best material they had. The New Stone Age began around _____ when farmers arrived in Britain. They brought _____ to sow, and animals, such as _____, _____ and _____. They lived mostly in small _____ huts with _____ roofs.

2 List as many things as you can which New Stone Age people could get from animals.

3 a) Draw the diagram of Grime's Graves mine.
b) How do you think the men lifted the flint up from the bottom of the mine? (Remember that they only had *natural* materials.)

4 a) Make an outline drawing of the house at Skara Brae (evidence A).
b) Mark on your drawing where you think these objects are: fireplace; stone-sided beds; open cupboard; tank.

5 Look at evidence B. What do you think a *pregnant* goddess was supposed to stand for?

9

3 Stonehenge and its Mysteries

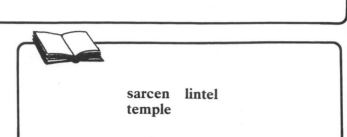

On Salisbury Plain, these people left behind their strangest monument. We call it Stonehenge. Over 4000 years ago, it began as a round ditch and bank. Bit by bit, people changed it over 1000 years to the shape it has today.

Yet it remains a mystery. Thousands of people may have helped to build Stonehenge but we do not know who they were; we are not even sure why they built it. The builders could not write so there is no record of what it was all about.

Inside the earth bank is a ring of 56 holes. Most of them contained burnt human bones. Inside this ring, people had started to build two rings of bluestones which came from South Wales.

Later, these were taken down and the holes filled in. Instead, people built another circle of 30 huge **sarcen** stones, weighing on average 28 tonnes each. Later, some of the bluestones were formed into a circle inside the sarcens, and others into a horseshoe shape.

That is what Stonehenge looks like today, but it explains none of its mysteries.

First, there is the problem of the bluestones. They came from South Wales. But how did they get to Salisbury Plain? Some people have suggested that the ice may have shifted them during the Ice Age. But no other bluestones have been found nearby. Some other people have said that they were brought by sea. It is possible, though difficult.

What is clear is that the builders must have been very keen on these stones, because other big stones could have been found nearby. What was so special about the bluestones? We just do not know.

Second, we are not certain how they raised the stones when they got them to Stonehenge. The upright stones were probably hauled on wooden rollers and then levered into a hole which had already been dug.

On top of the sarcens are fitted stones known as **lintels**. How they lifted them is a bigger mystery.

sarcen   lintel   temple

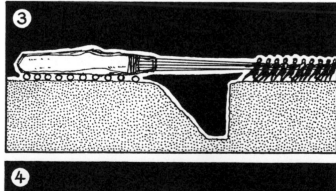

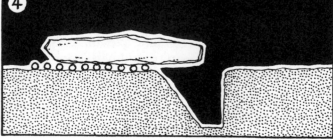

These pictures show one way in which the stones might have been raised. They do not show how the job was finished. (See question 2.)

10

One view is that they were gradually raised on piles of criss-crossed legs. Other people think it might have been done in winter when a snow ramp could have been built. But, again, no one is sure.

There is, anyway, an even bigger mystery! Why was Stonehenge built at all? It probably started as a meeting-place, but it became something far greater. It became a kind of **temple**, a temple which shows that New Stone Age people understood about the movements of the sun and moon.

For example, on Midsummer Day, the sun can be seen to rise over a special stone, called the Heelstone; on Midwinter Day, it shines through the gap between two upright stones. Stonehenge might have been built so that people could measure the seasons.

This would have been a major step forward. After all, these people were farmers. They needed to count the days if they were to sow their crops at the right times. If they were a week or so late, the crop might be ruined.

We shall never know all the answers to the riddle of Stonehenge. But we can see that it was a great achievement – and it seems to have brought people one step closer to controlling nature.

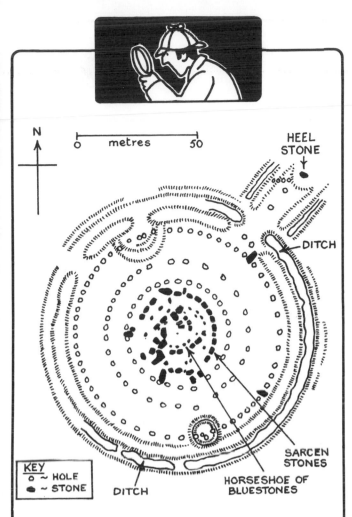

A A plan of Stonehenge.

B Part of Stonehenge today, showing sarcen stones and the Heelstone. On Midsummer Day the sun rises above the Heelstone.

1 Explain what each of the following has to do with Stonehenge: sarcen stones; bluestones; lintels; Midsummer Day.

2 Look at the pictures on page 10. Using the text to help you, draw pictures to show how people finished putting the upright stones in place.

3 a) Draw the plan of Stonehenge, shown above.
b) To get some idea of the size, make a chalk drawing of it on your school playground. Is it bigger or smaller than you thought it would be?
c) How many people do you think could get inside the outer circle?
d) Why do you think they used such large stones?

4 Write down each of the mysteries about Stonehenge. Choose any one of these and explain what *you* think the solution is.

4 People Begin Using Iron

People of the Iron Age. Background picture shows the Iron Age hut at Butser Farm in Hampshire.

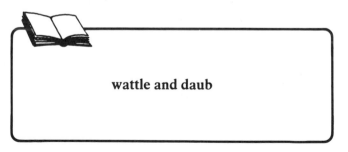

wattle and daub

By the time Stonehenge was finished, people had begun to use metal to make weapons. First, they used copper; then, they added tin to it to make bronze. Bronze was harder than copper but it bends easily and does not stay sharp for long.

The metal which replaced it gave its name to a new period of British history – the Iron Age. The first iron tools began to appear in about 700 BC, when the metal was first used by people called Celts.

The Celts had come from the European mainland. They were tall and fair, with blue eyes.

They wore their fair hair long and even rinsed it in lime to make it lighter. The men had long flowing moustaches; the women wore jewellery and used make-up made from berries and herbs.

Although we call this period the Iron Age, iron was not used by everyone straight away. For centuries, it was still a precious metal. But it did make a big difference to people's lives. Iron axes could cut down bigger trees; iron tools made building easier and an iron tip on the plough improved farming.

They still lived in huts made of **wattle and daub**. Often, there would be a group of these on a hilltop, surrounded by a ditch and earth bank to protect them. On the hillside, they made small square fields to grow their corn. Cattle and sheep were taken down to the valley to graze.

In a big village, there might be one larger hut, possibly used by the chief of the tribe. The hut shown on this page has been specially built in Hampshire, using the plan of an original Iron Age hut. It is surprisingly large: 200 trees were cut down for its posts and up to 200 people could sleep on the floor.

While the men were farming, the women were busy weaving cloth or making clothes. They liked brightly-coloured clothes and the men sometimes wore tight-fitting trousers. Otherwise, the women would be grinding corn or making bread.

Bread was their main food, along with porridge. They probably had this most days, although they ate meat as well. The main meat was beef, either roasted on a spit or boiled in an iron pot. Yet they must have taken care over their food. The men hated to get fat!

These people did not make up one nation, like Britain is today. People belonged to different tribes. In time, each tribe had its own king or queen, whom people had to obey. Each leader had warriors to fight for him or her. Towards the end of the Iron Age, these people were growing more warlike.

They needed to be. By then, the Romans were becoming interested in Britain.

1 Join up the words in list A with the descriptions in list B to make full sentences.

List A	*List B*
The Celts	bronze because it was harder.
Iron was better than	tribes, ruled by a king or queen.
They lived	first used iron in Britain.
These people belonged to	in huts made of wood, wattle and daub.

2 a) Draw the hut shown on page 12.
   b) What is the roof made from?
   c) On what special occasions might the chief have wanted to bring all his tribe together?

3 a) Look at evidence A, B and C. Write down what you think each object is.
   b) Draw two of the objects being used.

4 Iron had many other uses, besides those mentioned in the chapter. List as many uses as you can. For each one, explain why iron was a good material to use.

Three objects from the Iron Age.

A

B

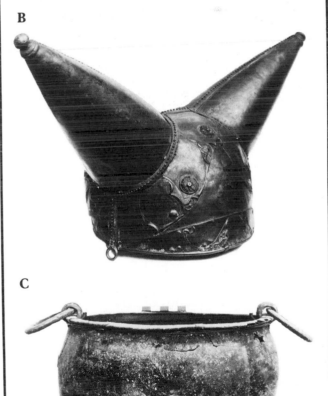

C

5 Living in 'the Iron Age'

quern

One daily job was making bread. The man on the right is using a quern to grind the corn.

A few years ago, a group of 12 adults and three children spent a whole year finding out what life in the Iron Age was like. A village just like an Iron Age one was built for them to live in.

It had a big round house where the group lived and slept, and smaller buildings for stores and materials. Around the village was a ditch and a fence, just as there would have been over 2000 years ago.

Experts told them how to do basic jobs, such as grinding corn, but they had to learn a lot for themselves. BBC Television filmed them during the year to make a record of how well they were coping.

They found the life very hard. It rained a great deal that year and the village was often a sea of mud. Their leather shoes let in water and they learned to tie wooden soles underneath them.

They kept animals similar to those which Iron Age people had. There were chickens, pigs, cows, geese and goats. The goats' milk was used to make cheese which they flavoured with herbs.

Bread was their main food. Every day, they ground 20 bowls of wheat to make flour for baking.

They did this in a stone quern, which is two large stones on top of each other. The corn was dropped in a hole at the top and the top stone turned by a handle. The flour was then mixed with hot water and salt (and, sometimes, sour milk, too) to make the dough. The dough was kneaded and, finally, baked in an oven.

They were not allowed to have matches so fires had to be started by rubbing wood together. After a while, they kept the fire in the round house going all the time.

Breakfast was cooked overnight. It was porridge made from boiled wheat, sweetened with honey. Other food included boiled beans, cheese and even leaves!

There was no sugar in the Iron Age, so these people had to use honey. That meant keeping their own bees. Some of the honey was used to make food, such as honey cakes.

Many other things which we take for granted they had to do without. There were no toothbrushes, so they used twigs instead. There was no soap powder, so clothes were just pounded in a tub full of water. And, of course, they were not allowed shampoos, so they rubbed clay in their hair

Looking after the pigs.

POUR THE GRAIN INTO THE HOLE AT THE TOP.

AT THE SAME TIME, TURN THE HANDLE TO MAKE THE TOP STONE TURN.

THE RESULT? FLOUR TO MAKE BREAD.

to get the dirt out. Then they had to wash the clay out!

There was always work to be done in the village. Everyone had a busy year, including the children. They soon learnt to help the adults with the day-to-day jobs. But they were not allowed to forget that they were really living in the 20th century. They still had to have school lessons!

Another job in the village.

Corn was ground into flour using a quern. It must have been slow and boring!

1   a) Make a list of the food which these people ate.
    b) Read the chapter again carefully. What *other* food could they have eaten? List as many kinds as you can.
2   a) Draw the picture of the stone quern.
    b) Write a paragraph to explain how it works.
3   These people did not really need a ditch or fence round their village, but Iron Age people did. Give two reasons why they would have needed them.
4   Write down all the *useful* things we have, which these people were not allowed (washing-up liquid, for instance!). Then, decide which you would have missed most and explain why.
5   These people gave up a year of their lives to live like this.
    a) Why do you think they did it?
    b) If *you* had the chance, would you spend a year living like this? Give details of your reasons for or against.

6 'Rome shall be the Capital of the World'

chariot arena
government
gladiator forum

A On the right, the ruins of the Roman Forum, at the heart of the city. There were temples and shops and **government** buildings, where people met to discuss the running of the Empire. The buildings of the Forum were copied in lands conquered by the Romans. (The picture above shows how it may have looked in ancient times.)

Nearly 2000 kilometres from Britain lies the city of Rome. At the time of the Iron Age in Britain, Rome was the biggest and finest city in the world.

Yet, in about 600 BC, it had just been a village on a hilltop in Italy. Over the next 600 years, Romans conquered much of Europe and part of North Africa. It became the greatest empire the world had ever seen.

Over a million people lived in Rome. Many of them enjoyed a standard of living which was good even by modern standards. The rich lived in fine palaces and large houses while arches and monuments reminded Romans of their city's great achievements.

It was a busy, bustling city. The noise was tremendous and went on day and night. In the early morning, wooden carts trundled through the streets, bringing goods to the markets and shops.

And just about anything could be bought. Goods came from every part of the Empire. There were even ostrich feathers from Africa on sale!

The shops were mostly small, but many other public buildings were huge, even by modern standards. They included free public baths, where there were large rooms in which people could relax and gossip about the Empire's news.

If they preferred, they could go to an inn or eating shop, or just sit in one of the city's many parks.

If it was a holiday, the Romans would probably be looking for entertainment. There were theatres, and **arenas** where they could watch contests between wild animals or fighters called gladiators. Or there were **chariot** races at the race-track. It was all so different from Iron Age Britain.

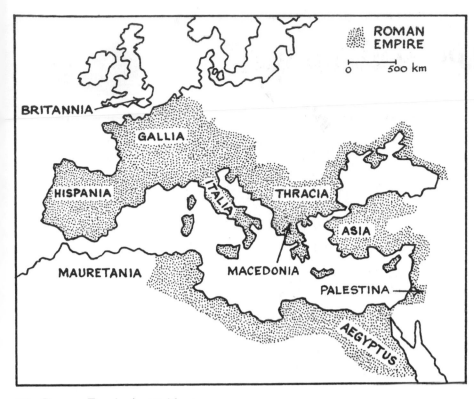

The Roman Empire in AD 14.

Roman statues sometimes had separate hair so that it could be changed to fit the latest fashions.

So were the houses. Rich people had large houses with stone floors and paintings on the walls. Water was piped to the house, so there was a lavatory and drains to carry away waste water. Some houses even had a kind of central heating, and the family had warm water for washing.

Rich children spent their days at school. They were taught how to read and write. The boys also learned how to fight. Many armies were needed to control such a great empire.

Unlike the muddy villages of Britain, Rome had proper streets, often paved with stone. Walk down one and you might have seen people from all over Europe – slaves, businessmen or just people out shopping. Every day, street cleaners went round to sweep away the rubbish.

Of course, not every Roman was rich. In fact, most of them were not. Thousands of poor people lived in dirty, unhealthy blocks of flats. They were overcrowded and dangerous. There was no street lighting and it was not safe in these slum areas after dark.

Yet it *was* the most advanced city of the age. And, wherever the Romans went, they built towns and cities like Rome itself. They built them in North Africa and in Europe. Eventually, Britain, too, would be shaped on Roman lines. But, first, the Romans had to beat the Britons.

1   Divide your page into two columns. At the top of one, write *Iron Age Britain*; at the top of the other, write *Rome*. Now, list the differences between the two places. Read the last few pages again, if necessary. You should be able to think of at least ten differences.

2   a) Draw the map of the Roman Empire.
    b) Using an atlas, write down the modern names of the countries in the Empire.

3   a) How many people lived in ancient Rome?
    b) In the library, find out which British cities *today* have more people in them than Rome did then.

4   Evidence A shows the remains of the Roman forum. Do you think it would be better if it were rebuilt so people could see exactly what it looked like? Give reasons for your view.

javelin cavalry
standard-bearer
Emperor Legion

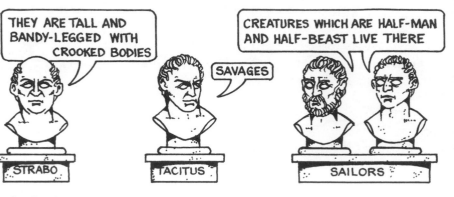

THEY ARE TALL AND BANDY-LEGGED WITH CROOKED BODIES

STRABO

CREATURES WHICH ARE HALF-MAN AND HALF-BEAST LIVE THERE

SAVAGES

TACITUS

SAILORS

What the Romans thought of the Britons.

By 55 BC, a Roman army was fighting in Gaul. The war was a tough one and the Roman leader, Julius Caesar, heard that the Gauls had been getting help from the Britons. He decided that he would teach the Britons a lesson.

He gathered 12 000 men and set sail for Britain one day late in August. He arrived early the next morning to find the Dover cliffs guarded by armed men. So he sailed down the coast to find a new landing-place for his ships, just 11 kilometres away.

But the Britons had been following and were waiting for the Romans. British chariots charged towards them, while **javelins** and stones rained down on the Romans.

The **standard-bearer** of the 10th **Legion** saved the day. He jumped into the water, carrying the standard, and the men followed. Plunging through the water, they drove back the Britons who eventually made a run for it.

Roman soldiers meet British warriors in 55 BC.

It was not Caesar's greatest victory. The ships bringing his **cavalry** were caught in a storm and had to sail back to Gaul. Next, the high tide wrecked some of his ships. They quickly repaired some of the rest and took prisoners on board. Then, they were off and glad to be back in Gaul for the winter.

But Caesar could not leave it at that. Next year, he was back. This time, he brought 30 000 men. The Britons were impressed and did not try to stop him landing. This time, the Roman soldiers marched far inland and, one by one, forced the British tribes to make peace.

Meanwhile, the Gauls were getting restless now that so many Roman soldiers were in Britain. It was not much good Caesar conquering Britain if he was going to lose Gaul. So, with yet more prisoners, he sailed late one evening for Gaul. He never returned.

Of course, Caesar got credit for beating the British but the victory did not count for much. For over 90 years, the Roman armies left Britain alone.

But traders came, bringing luxury goods for the Britons, and they took back to Rome stories of how rich these islands were.

In the meantime, Roman **Emperors** sometimes made plans to conquer Britain and add it to their Empire. But it was AD 43 before one of them got round to it. A new Emperor, Claudius, saw his chance to win a great victory. It was too good a chance to miss.

He sent a huge force of about 40 000 men. There were four legions in all and many cavalry. This time, they had picked a safe harbour well in advance.

Some tribes made peace quickly but others fought hard. One bitter battle lasted two days. Claudius himself turned up afterwards with more men and even a few elephants. It was just the first of a whole range of new things the Romans had in store for the Britons.

Claudius himself stayed only 16 days before going back to Rome in triumph. But the fighting went on for some years. And the legions stayed.

1 Copy out and complete this paragraph:
Julius _____ first came to Britain in
——BC. Although he won a victory, his _____
were badly damaged and he soon returned to
_____. He came back in —— BC with more
men but the _____ were becoming restless and
Caesar had to return there to keep them under
control.

2 Why do you think Claudius brought elephants with him?

3 Read evidence A and B.
a) In evidence A, what advantages did the Britons have over the Romans?
b) In evidence B, three things prove that the Britons had practised this sort of attack. What are they?
c) Using evidence A, list the problems which the Romans faced.
d) Which of these problems do you think Caesar should have foreseen?

4 Using the text and evidence A, describe in your own words the landing in 55 BC. Write it as if you were one of the Roman soldiers.

A Julius Caesar described how the Britons fought when his men landed in 55 BC:

The Romans were faced with serious problems. The soldiers were not familiar with the ground and had their hands full, weighed down by the heavy weight of their weapons and armour. Yet they were supposed to jump down, keep on their feet in the waves and fight the enemy.

However, the enemy was standing on dry land or only going a short way into the water; they were fighting with their limbs free of equipment on ground they knew well. They boldly threw javelins and galloped their horses which were trained for this sort of work.

These dangers frightened our soldiers, who were not used to battles of this kind, with the result that they did not show the same speed and enthusiasm as they usually did in battles on dry land.

B Caesar described how the Britons used chariots:

Chariots are used like this. First of all, the charioteers drive all over the field hurling javelins. Generally the horses and the noise of the wheels are enough to terrify the enemy and throw them into confusion. As soon as they have got through the cavalry, the warriors jump down from their chariots and fight on foot.

Meanwhile, the charioteers then move away and place their chariots in such a way that the warriors can easily get back to them if they are hard pressed by the size of the enemy.

So they combine the easy movement of cavalry with the staying-power of foot-soldiers. Regular practice makes them so skilful that they can control their horses at a full gallop, even on a steep slope. And they can stop and turn them in a moment. The warriors can run along the chariot pole, stand on the yoke and get back into the chariot as quick as lightning.

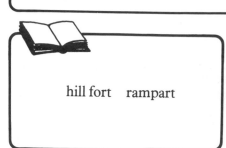

8 Attacking a Hill Fort

hill fort   rampart

Looking down on the huge Iron Age hill fort at Maiden Castle in Dorset.

Look at any map of southern England and you will notice that ancient forts are quite common. In fact, there are over 3000 of them. They were made of earth and usually built on hilltops. There, an Iron Age tribe could come together in safety.

If the Romans were to conquer Britain, they would have to attack and capture these forts. One of the four legions which landed in AD 43 was the 2nd Legion, commanded by General Vespasian.

His job was to conquer the south and west of the country and he had to attack 20 of these hill forts. One of the largest was Maiden Castle in Dorset.

It was built with three large earth banks, called ramparts, around a flat space where the Britons lived. The ramparts were steep, making them difficult to attack. At the east and west ends were gateways guarded by high stone walls.

Because the entrances were the weakest points, the ramparts were carefully built up to form long passages. Attackers had to go along these, fighting every inch of the way. Meanwhile, the defenders stood on the ramparts and slung stones at them.

Perhaps this does not sound as dangerous as being attacked by spears. But stones can kill, and a good slinger could kill someone up to 60 metres away.

Capturing Maiden Castle meant a fierce battle. Why didn't the Romans just go round it and ignore it? The reason was that it was defended by a tribe called the Durotriges. When other tribes made peace with the Romans, the Durotriges fought on. It was their main hill fort and Vespasian had to destroy it.

We cannot be sure how he went about it. But the evidence seems to show that he attacked the East Gate. Arrows, spears and stones were all fired into the fort. The East Gate itself was destroyed and huts outside it were burned down.

It was a bitter fight and no one showed any pity. Even women and children who had come into the fort for protection were killed. The bodies were quickly buried in shallow graves, along with a bowl and some food. Some of the bodies were even hacked about after being killed.

20

The fort was badly damaged, although the Britons went on living there for some years. Only later did they move to a new town which we now call Dorchester.

And Vespasian? He fought 30 battles before returning to Rome. His victories made him famous and, years later, he became emperor.

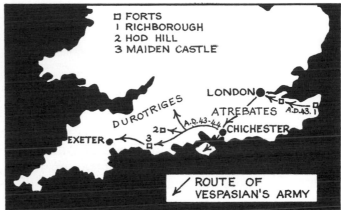

Map showing where Vespasian's army went.

1 Explain the meaning of each of these words: hill fort; rampart; legion.

2 Copy out and complete this paragraph:
   The 2nd Legion was commanded by _____. He conquered the _____ part of the country and attacked 20 _____, including _____ Castle in Dorset.

3 a) Trace the diagram of the east entrance of Maiden Castle.
   b) Imagine you are Vespasian. You must decide how to attack the fort. (Remember that the defenders' sling shots can reach up to 60 metres.) Mark on your route in colour. Also, mark in five spots where you expect the Britons to put their best stone slingers. (Use an X for each spot.)

4 Look at evidence A. Apart from skeletons, what else can you see in the graves? Why do you think they were put there?

5 Why do you think the bodies were attacked *after* the people had been killed?

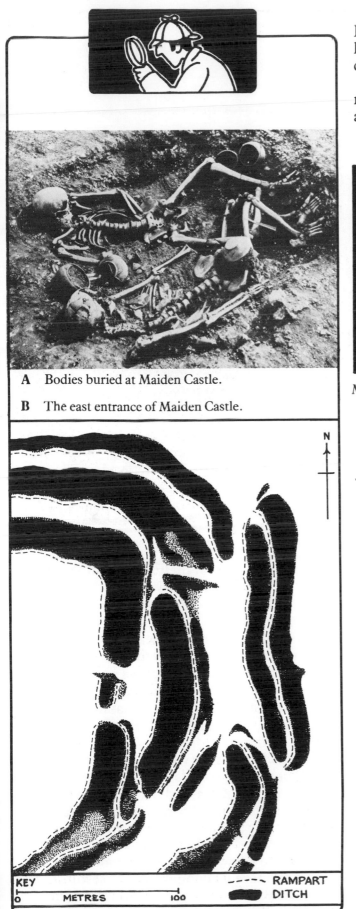

A Bodies buried at Maiden Castle.

B The east entrance of Maiden Castle.

KEY

0 — METRES — 100

- - - - RAMPART

▬▬ DITCH

9 The Roman Army

frontier stirrup
vine-staff
legionary auxiliary
centurion

The Roman soldiers who attacked Maiden Castle were part of the best fighting force in the world. It took about 55 000 of them to defend Britain.

The Roman army was made up of two separate groups. The more important soldiers were the legionaries. There were about 5500 of them serving in each army as foot-soldiers. Each was a Roman citizen and served for up to 25 years.

The other group was the auxiliaries. They were people who belonged to tribes which the Romans had beaten. They were usually sent into battle first, before the legionaries. Many of them were archers or cavalry; others tended to do the rougher jobs, such as guarding **frontier** forts.

The cavalry was a key part of the Roman army and was a frightening sight, charging down upon the enemy. But riders did have one problem. The **stirrup** had not yet been invented and the cavalrymen must have found it hard to control their horses.

Each group of 80 men was under the control of a centurion. These centurions were the real leaders in the Roman army. They were tough, trained soldiers who had usually worked their way up to become officers. Each centurion carried a **vine-staff** as a sign of his power to beat any man who did not do his job properly.

Sometimes, the soldiers had very little to do. Men spent their time in their barracks, doing repairs and generally cleaning up. But an attack might come at any time so soldiers had to be ready. And they had to be fit. They went everywhere on foot and had to be ready to march up to 32 kilometres in a day, carrying 27 kilos of equipment, as well as their weapons.

Training was hard. They had to cope with 'obstacle courses', wearing full armour, as well as mock battles and route marches. Even cutting

A ROMAN SOLDIER CARRIED....

BRONZE HELMET

BODY ARMOUR

SWORD

TWO JAVELINS

GRAIN TO LAST 15 DAYS

BASKET

PERSONAL POSSESSIONS

COOKING POT

AN AXE

A PICK

SHIELD

TWO WOODEN POSTS TO MAKE A FENCE THAT NIGHT...AND A SPADE TO DIG THE HOLES.

A Roman soldier did not travel light!

down trees was part of their training programme. It was a long training and discipline was harsh. A soldier could be stoned to death if he did not do his duty properly.

It was this training and discipline which made the Roman army so good. It was done to make sure that, in battle, the army fought as one man. Most fighting was hand-to-hand and could get very bloody. Officers had to be sure that no one would back away at the last moment. Everyone had to fight his hardest.

Rewards for bravery were given to encourage them. There were medals and neck-chains, and a crown of oak leaves was given to anyone who saved another soldier's life. There were also rewards for the first man to attack the walls of a fort or board an enemy's ship.

But, while a few gained great honours, there were many more who fought and were killed. The soldiers in Britain were soon to find that some Britons would not surrender without a fight.

Left and centre: two Roman soldiers. (See question 2.) On the right is a standard-bearer. His job was to carry the legion's standard into battle.

A A writer called Vegetius produced an army handbook in the 4th century AD. This was his advice to people choosing new soldiers:

Those choosing new recruits should be careful to examine their faces, their eyes and the shape of their limbs and to see that they are likely to make good soldiers. For experts have shown that choosing men is just like choosing horses and dogs.

A young soldier should have alert eyes and should hold his head upright. The recruit should be broad-chested with powerful shoulders and brawny arms. His fingers should be long rather than short. He should not be pot-bellied or have a fat bottom. His calves and feet should not be flabby; they should be made entirely of tough sinew.

When you find all these qualities in a recruit, you can afford to take him even if he is a little on the short side. It is better for soldiers to be strong rather than tall.

The well-being of the Roman state depends on the recruits you choose; so you must choose men who are outstanding not only in body but in mind.

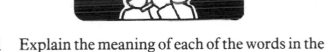

1 Explain the meaning of each of the words in the word box.
2 a) Draw the outline figures of the legionary and the centurion.
   b) Decide which is which, then name them.
   c) On your drawings, label these items: shield; leather sandals; helmet; javelin; vine-staff; sword; dagger; armour.
   d) Write a paragraph about each man to describe his job.
3 In your own words, explain why the standard-bearer was so important. (Read page 18 first.)
4 a) Read evidence A.
   b) List the qualities which this writer thinks are necessary in a new soldier.
   c) Choose the *one* thing you think is most important and give reasons for your choice.
   d) Do you think the writer has missed anything out?

10 The Druids

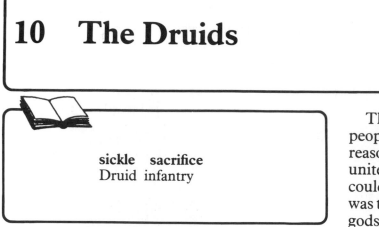

sickle   sacrifice
Druid   infantry

ANGLESEY

Anglesey was a main Druid base.

The Romans had no intention of becoming friendly with one group. These were the Druids. They had met the Druids even before Caesar attacked Britain because there were also Druids in western Europe.

The Druids were Iron Age priests whom the Britons feared and respected. They were also teachers and judges who knew the laws and customs of the tribes. As well as being experts on the past, they could foretell the future.

A man might take up to 20 years to become a Druid. By then, his knowledge would have been enormous, yet we know little about what his knowledge was. The reason is that they were not allowed to write any of it down.

But we do know something about their religious ceremonies. They were held in secret places in forests, well away from villages. An oak tree with mistletoe growing on it was an ideal place. They thought that mistletoe was holy.

A Roman writer watched one of these ceremonies. He saw a Druid, dressed all in white, climb the oak tree and cut some mistletoe with a golden **sickle**. Then, two white bulls were killed as a **sacrifice** before feasting began.

The Druids could travel anywhere because people respected them, so the Romans had good reason to be nervous about them. If anyone could unite the Britons against the Romans, the Druids could. But what really made the Romans hate them was that the Druids sacrificed human beings to the gods. The Romans had once done this themselves but, now that they had stopped, they wanted everyone else to stop too.

In AD 54, the Emperor Claudius finally banned the Druids. In AD 60, the new British governor decided to attack the Druid centre on Anglesey. He built boats for his infantry, who were the foot-soldiers, while the cavalry swam their horses across from the mainland.

Waiting for them, they found Druids dressed in white and women dressed in black, shouting and cursing them. For a moment, the Romans hesitated. Then, they advanced and wiped out the Druids. To be on the safe side, the Romans then destroyed the Druids' sacred meeting-places.

It was a successful campaign for the Romans, but their troubles were not over. While they were in Anglesey, they got news of an even greater threat. There was a revolt – and it was led by a woman.

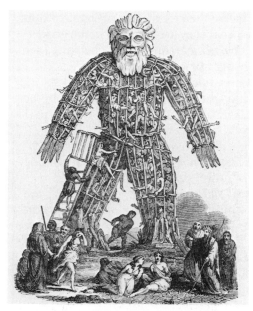

Caesar described Druid sacrifices. This is what an artist thinks one may have looked like.

24

A Julius Caesar wrote about the Druids in about 52 BC:

The Gauls are extremely superstitious. So people suffering from serious diseases, as well as those who are to do battle, offer human sacrifices. They use Druids to perform this task. They believe that the only way of saving a man's life is to satisfy the god's anger by giving another life in its place. They have regular state sacrifices of the same kind.

Some tribes have huge figures made of wickerwork and fill the limbs with living men. They are set on fire and burned to death. They think the gods prefer them to execute guilty men but when they run short of criminals, they make up with innocent men.

B A Greek writer called Strabo described them in about 8 BC:

They include men who write verses, called bards. They sing to instruments similar to lyres. The Druids are believed to be most upright and so they settle public and private arguments. On some occasions, they decide on battles and stop the fighters the night beforehand.

They wear gold. They have gold collars on their necks and bracelets on their arms and wrists. Some persons are dressed in dyed clothes embroidered with gold.

C Another writer described them in about 44 BC:

They have a strange custom. Having got a man to be sacrificed, they hit him with a sword on a place above the diaphragm. When the victim has fallen, they work out from the way he fell and the flow of his blood what may happen in the future.

Both in peace and war, friends and enemies alike listen to their opinion and to that of those who write the verses. Often during a battle, when armies are approaching each other, these men rush between them and put an end to the fighting, taming the fighters as if they were wild beasts.

1 Copy out this grid and fill it in, using the clues below.

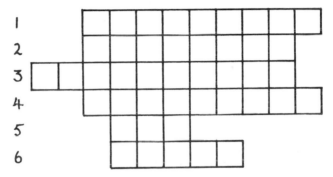

1 Killing an animal or person for the gods.
2 Emperor who banned the Druid religion.
3 Where modern Druids meet at Midsummer.
4 The Druids thought this plant was holy.
5 The tree on which the 'holy' plant grew.
6 An Iron Age priest.
Now, write down the name which reads down. What did he think of the Druids?

2 Read all the evidence and text carefully. Make a list of all the things the Druids were supposed to do. For each one, explain what harm or good it may have done.

3 Imagine you were the Roman governor who decided to kill the Druids. Write a short speech which you will make to your troops, explaining why the Druids must be killed.

4 a) What reasons are there for being careful about accepting what Caesar says about the Druids?
b) Do *you* think the Romans were right to destroy them? Give reasons for your answer.

Midsummer morning at Stonehenge. Every year, modern Druids come to celebrate Midsummer Day. But the Druids were most important long after Stonehenge was finished and there is no reason to assume it had anything to do with them.

11　A Queen Called Boudica

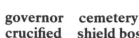

IT IS WINTER IN AD 60. THE ROMANS ARE FACING A NEW REVOLT, THIS TIME BY THE ICENI TRIBE WHO LIVE IN EAST ANGLIA. BUT THIS REVOLT IS RATHER SPECIAL. ITS LEADER IS A WOMAN OF ABOUT 40, THE QUEEN OF THE ICENI, AND SHE IS THE FIRST WOMAN IN BRITISH HISTORY WHOSE NAME WE KNOW. SHE IS CALLED BOUDICA.

Boudica's husband had died and had given his kingdom to the Roman Emperor and his two daughters. The result was that Roman soldiers moved in. They looted the kingdom and took his relatives as slaves. Boudica herself said she had been flogged and her daughters assaulted.

The Iceni decided to fight back and other East Anglian tribes joined them. Put together, they made a huge force of at least 30 000 people but they were not as well organised as the Romans. Although some had spears and swords, others only had sticks. A Roman army might have defeated them quite quickly.

But the Romans had a problem. Their **governor**, Suetonius, was away in Anglesey and there were no legions close at hand. So the rebel army looted its way south towards the great Roman city of Colchester.

Inside the city, the people had strange warnings. Dreadful moans were heard and, out at sea, a blood-red stain was seen. Soon it was all too real. Boudica's revolt.

An artist's idea of Queen Boudica.

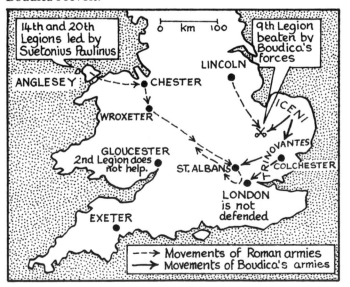

The rebels surrounded the town and simply burned it down. The survivors tried to hold out in the temple; they lasted just two days before it, too, was captured. Every man, woman and child was killed. Out in the **cemetery**, the tombstones were smashed up.

Outside the town, the rebels fought and destroyed the 9th Legion which had come to stop them. Only the Roman cavalry escaped. Probably about 2000 legionaries were killed.

London was the richest prize of all but Suetonius decided that he just could not defend the town. So the tiny Roman army was ordered to leave and the tribespeople moved in. Their revenge was dreadful. They looted the houses and hacked the inhabitants to pieces. Over 70 000 were killed: some were hung or burned; others were **crucified** and left to die.

Everything was going the tribespeople's way. But Boudica's greatest test was still to come.

A The only accounts of Boudica's revolt were written by Romans. The most reliable was this one, written by Tacitus:

Suetonius collected together the 14th Legion and some of the 20th Legion, with some auxiliaries from nearby. In all, there were nearly 10 000 armed men. He chose to attack without delay.

He chose a position which was approached by a narrow valley and with a wood behind him. In front of him was open country so he could not be ambushed. He drew up his legions in close order, with auxiliaries beside them and cavalry on the wings.

The Britons were dotted all over the place and dashing around. There were more of them than ever before. They were so sure of winning that they brought their wives along to watch. They were in waggons at the edge of the battlefield.

Boudica drove all round the tribes in a chariot with her daughters. 'We Britons are used to woman commanders,' she cried. 'But I am not fighting for my lost freedom and to avenge my daughters. The gods will give us our just revenge.

'You must either win this battle or die. That is what I, a woman, plan to do. Let the men live as slaves, if they wish.'

Meanwhile, Suetonius told his men:

'Ignore their roars and empty threats. They've got more women than men, and have no weapons. Just keep close together and throw your javelins. Knock them down with your **shield bosses** and kill them with your swords. Forget about looting: when you have won, everything will be yours.'

The battle started. The legions stood where they were. When the enemy came forward, they threw their javelins and then rushed forward, forming a wedge shape. The auxiliaries and cavalry followed. They broke down all who resisted them.

The rest of the Britons fled but the line of waggons blocked their way. The troops showed no mercy, even to the women.

It was a great victory. One report said that nearly 80 000 Britons died but we only lost about 400 men, with the same number injured. Boudica poisoned herself. The Commander of the 2nd Legion stabbed himself to death when he heard of the other legions' success because, by refusing to join Suetonius, he had cheated his men of their share of the victory.

B Dio Cassius described what Boudica looked like. He was writing over 100 years after she died:

Boudica was much more intelligent than women usually are. She was very tall and looked terrifying, with a fierce glint in her eyes and a harsh voice. A great mass of startling yellow hair hung down to her hips. Around her neck she had a huge **torque** of gold and she wore a dress of many colours with a thin cloak over it, pinned together with a brooch.

1   Match up the descriptions on the left with the correct names from the right:

East Anglian tribe	Iceni
the Roman governor	Boudica
Queen of the Iceni tribe	Colchester
important Roman city	Suetonius

2   a) Why did the Iceni revolt?
    b) Why couldn't Suetonius fight the Iceni at the start?

3   a) Read evidence A. Describe (i) Boudica's tactics and (ii) Suetonius' tactics.
    b) Whose tactics were better? Give as many reasons as possible for your answer.

4   All the information on these two pages comes from Roman writers, mostly Tacitus. Is there anything you do *not* believe? If so, write it down and explain why.

5   Imagine you were a reporter at this battle. Write down the questions you would want to ask Suetonius and what you think his answers would have been.

6   Using evidence A and B, draw Boudica talking to her troops before the battle.

Picts

The 9th Legion had been badly beaten by Boudica's army but it was brought up to full strength again. In later years, it was moved north into the front line of defence against the Britons.

For most of this time it was based at York. But, some time before AD 122, it left Britain. People used to think that it had disappeared altogether but we now think that it probably went across to Europe.

But something *had* happened. A later writer said there had been a serious rebellion in Britain at about this time. Many Roman soldiers were killed. Perhaps the 9th Legion had not done its job properly; maybe it had left in disgrace.

Anyway, its place was taken by the 6th Legion in about AD 122. And the new legion certainly had plenty of work to do. One of its first jobs was to help build a huge wall across the country.

It was the Emperor Hadrian's idea. Its aim was simple. It was to keep the Picts out of Roman Britain. The result was the greatest military building anywhere in the Empire – 117 kilometres long and 6.5 metres high. The top was wide enough for two soldiers to do sentry duty side by side.

Of course, the Romans needed more than a wall. They needed somewhere to keep the soldiers who were going to guard it. So every 8 kilometres along it they built a big fort, where about 500 men were stationed. And every 1500 metres there was a smaller fort for about 30 men.

The legionaries built all this themselves. It was just another of the many jobs for which they were trained. Each block of stone on the outside of the wall was carefully shaped by hand. When they came to marshy ground, turf was used instead of stone.

Three times the Picts almost destroyed the wall and it had to be rebuilt. But for about 250 years it was guarded constantly – a lonely outpost for thousands of men on the very edge of a great empire.

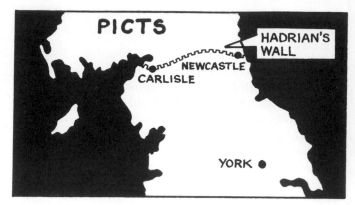

Map showing Hadrian's Wall. The people living to the north of it were called Picts.

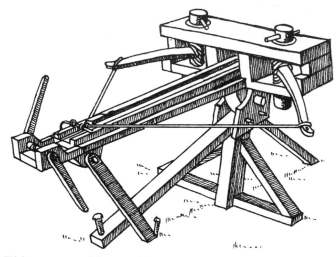

This was a machine used by the Romans when attacking a fort. It is a ballista and it fired a bolt which could pierce armour up to 300 metres away.

LET'S HOPE HE DOESN'T WANT AN EXTENSION!

A Emperor Hadrian made this speech to some other soldiers building a wall in AD 128:

You built the defences in a single day, while others would have spread the work over several days. It took you as long to build a wall out of heavy stones as most troops would take to build a wall of light, easy-to-handle, turf. You dug a trench in a straight line through hard gravel and trimmed it smooth.

When this was done, you went into the camp, collected your food, collected your weapons and then followed the cavalry out of the camp, as if ready for battle.

He also told the cavalry:

You have done the hardest thing of all, throwing javelins when wearing full armour. Your jumping was lively today; yesterday, it was swift. If you had not done everything properly, I would have told you. I would also have said if you had done something very well. But it was the fact that your performance was consistent which pleased me.

B Tools used by the Romans:

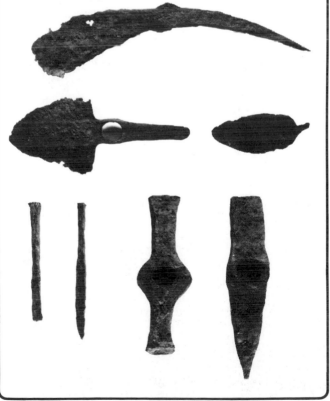

What the Wall probably looked like when it was new.

1 Match up the names on the left with the correct description from the right:

Hadrian   people living north of the wall
the Picts   Emperor who built the wall
York   mysteriously left Britain
9th Legion   the 9th Legion's base

2 Explain clearly why the wall was built.

3 a) Draw the map showing Hadrian's Wall.
b) The Romans later built another wall. In your library, find out where this was, then draw it on your map and name it.

4 a) Read evidence A. Was Hadrian pleased with these soldiers? Pick out those words which show that he was or was not pleased.
b) What does this speech tell you about Roman soldiers?

5 a) Look at evidence B. It shows tools used to build the wall. Draw these in your book.
b) Beside each tool, write its correct name. Choose the names from this list: pickaxe; chisel; hammer; trowel; tool for digging trenches.

13 The Romans Build Roads

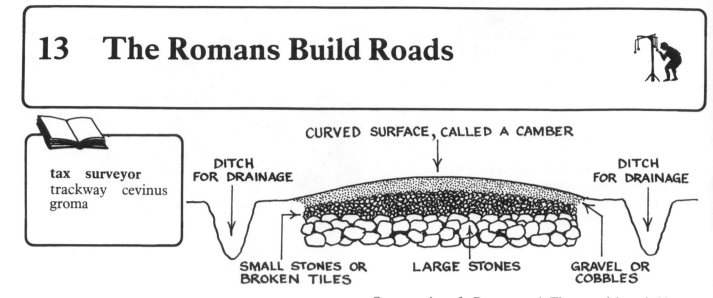

tax   surveyor
trackway   cevinus
groma

Cross-section of a Roman road. The materials varied but there were always stones at the bottom. Only the best roads had stone slabs on the surface.

The Romans needed to move their armies round the country quickly to keep the Britons under control. When they first arrived, Roman troops used the old trackways which the Britons themselves used. These ran along the high ground and often took people out of their way.

The Romans needed something better because roads were more important to them than to the Britons. Good roads meant more trade. And more trade meant more **taxes** for the Emperor. He also needed roads to send messages. After all, the whole Empire was run from Rome and that was nearly 2000 kilometres from Britain.

But, above all, it was the Roman army which needed good, straight roads. So the army built them. In fact, they were not perfectly straight. They zig-zagged up hills and often avoided obstacles, but long stretches did run straight. Yet the Romans had no compasses or maps, so how did they do it?

The main roads of Roman Britain. (See evidence A and question 4.)

Roman **surveyors** used an instrument called a groma. It was a pair of boards fastened together into a cross shape. Lines with weights were hung from each corner so the surveyor could get a straight line by looking through them. In forest areas, they built fires in a straight line and used the smoke as markers.

Next, wooden posts marked out the line of the road and ditches were dug on each side to act as

The groma was used to make sure the road was straight.

drains. Often, the earth from these was used for the road, so that it was higher than the ground nearby. The legionaries did most of the building and used whatever materials they could get locally.

These new roads were always busy. Officials sometimes travelled in a cevinus, which was a kind of light chariot which only carried the driver. They could change horses about every 16 kilometres and stop for food and drink at one of the inns. These were roughly 48 kilometres apart.

Most people travelled on foot. Even poor merchants went from town to town with their goods strapped in packs on their backs. A better-off trader would travel on horseback or in a carriage. His goods would go by waggon, along with his slaves.

These waggons were probably the most common vehicle on a Roman road. In fact, most roads were built wide enough for two big four-wheeled heavy waggons to pass side by side without having to stop. But they were slow and clumsy; some towns wouldn't let them in.

The Romans had built the first real roads the country had ever seen. They were also very safe and fast to travel on. Yet, after the Romans left, they were allowed to fall into decay. It says a lot about how good they were that, a thousand years later, the Roman roads were still the best that Britain had.

The Saxons allowed the Roman roads to decay. This cartoon shows some of the reasons why.

A Henry of Huntingdon wrote in the 12th century about the Roman roads:

The safety of Britain was so important that they built four great highways from one end of the island to the other. They were military roads, in case of invasion.

The first runs from east to west and is called Ichenild. The second runs from south to north and is called Erninge Strate. The third crosses the island from south-east to north-west and is called Watling Street. The fourth is longer than the others and runs from Cornwall to Scotland. It runs from south-west to north-east and is called the Foss-way.

1 Explain the meaning of each of these words: groma; cevinus; trackway; surveyor; legionary.
2 a) Draw the cross-section of a Roman road.
   b) Write down *three* features which made this road such a good one.
3 a) List the reasons why Romans needed good roads.
   b) Which reason do you think was most important? Give reasons for your answer.
4 a) Draw the map of Roman roads on page 30.
   b) Read evidence A. Try to work out which road on the map is which. (The writer may not be quite right.)
5 a) Why do you think the Romans built roads wide enough for two waggons to pass without stopping?
   b) Waggon wheels were 1.42 metres apart. How wide do you think the roads needed to be?
6 a) Draw the groma on page 30.
   b) You can easily make one of these. A broom handle can be used for the pole and lumps of plasticene on the end of string make good weighted lines to hang down. If you make more than one, you can try them out.

basilica

No one is sure how many people lived in Roman Britain. These are just some estimates. Most experts today think that the figure should be higher, rather than lower.

The Romans also set about building towns. This was partly because they thought that people could only lead the best sort of life if they lived in towns. But they did have another good reason. Towns made it easier to control the Britons.

The Romans needed the help of the Britons in the day-to-day running of the country. After all, out of all the people in Britain, only about 100 000 had been brought in by the Romans. And half of these were soldiers. So, at most, there were just 50 000 Romans to run the country. They just could not do it unless the Britons helped.

So the Romans moved some native tribes down from their hilltops and into new towns, such as St Albans. They had done it before, when they conquered Spain and Gaul. They knew it would work.

These towns were planned in the days when the Romans thought their Empire would last for ever. So, inside the walls, they left plenty of space for more houses to be built later.

Like our modern towns, they grew bit by bit. But it did not happen by chance. The Romans believed in planning. Right from the start, the roads were laid out in neat, straight lines, criss-crossing each other at right angles.

Even so, Roman towns were small by modern standards. Most were really just large villages. Despite that, they *were* towns – and the Britons had never seen anything like them.

Some Roman towns were built around army bases. One of these was Colchester. It was chosen partly because it was the centre of the local British tribe. When the legion moved out in AD 49, the town council drew up a plan for the town. It was based partly on the layout of the old fort.

The army's influence stayed strong. The town council was made up of ex-soldiers and each one was given town land to build himself a home. About 400 square kilometres of land outside the town were also taken away from the tribespeople for the new townsfolk. Although it was a town, most people were still busy farming.

Strong walls and soldiers on the gates meant that the Romans could keep out anyone they did not want.

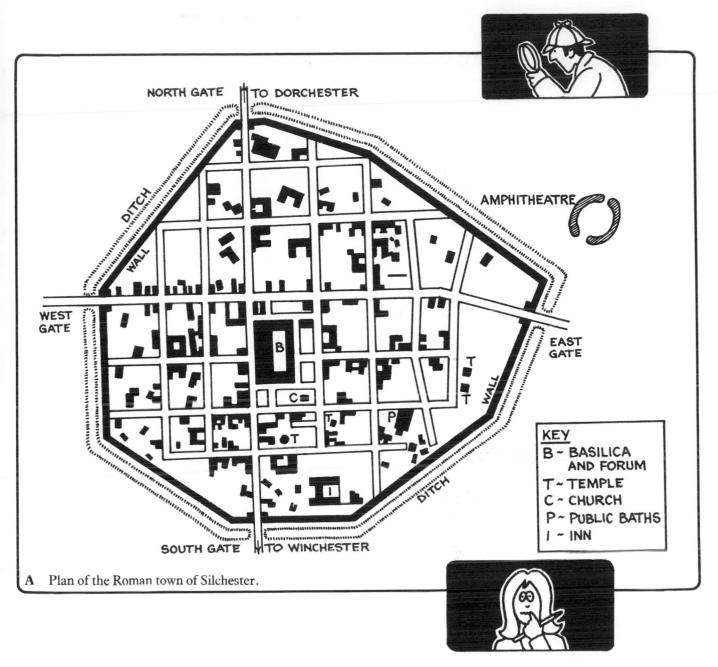

A Plan of the Roman town of Silchester.

1 Write out this paragraph, choosing the correct words from the brackets:

The Romans built towns because they thought towns were the (best/worst) places to live in but they were also useful for controlling the (Britains/Britons). Roman towns were carefully planned, with roads laid out in neat, (curved/straight) lines. There was usually plenty of (clean/open) space for more building later on.

2 a) Draw the plan of Silchester shown above.
b) In what ways was the town defended?
c) How can you tell that there were some Christians living there?

d) If you could choose to build a house there, which spot would you pick? Mark your site on the plan in a different colour and give reasons for your choice.

3 Read all page 34 before answering this question.
a) The picture at the top of page 34 is based on the plan shown lower down. Draw the plan in your book.
b) Using the text on the picture, name the places numbered 1 to 3 on the plan.

4 Why do you think it is so difficult to work out how many people lived in Roman Britain? Why should our guesses keep changing?

What the forum at Silchester looked like.

Usually, a wall of wood or stone was built around the town to protect it. Traffic in and out of town had to go through large gateways.

But, at Colchester, the council made a mistake. After destroying the defences of the old fort, they did not build new ones. They must have regretted this when Boudica's followers attacked the town in AD 60.

In the middle of each Roman town was a big open space called the forum. The important buildings, such as the town hall and law courts, were built here. It was also the main meeting-place and the centre of town life.

The main attractions were the shops which sold goods brought from all over the Empire. On market days, there were also traders selling goods from stalls. It was a busy, noisy place where people made speeches in the open air or just sat in a café, having a drink or snack.

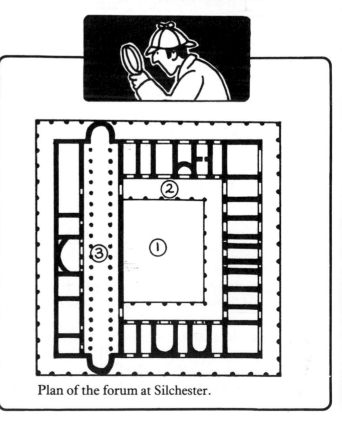

Plan of the forum at Silchester.

Revision

1 This square includes some hidden words. They are all words which have appeared in the word boxes so far. They could read up, down, sideways or diagonally. Each time you find a word, write it down and write one sentence about it.

R	B	A	M	I	S	S	I	O	N
O	F	R	A	M	O	R	G	D	L
T	N	E	M	U	N	O	M	H	I
A	L	N	M	M	S	J	U	N	N
I	N	A	O	E	U	Q	R	O	T
D	P	S	T	C	I	P	O	I	E
A	R	A	H	N	K	C	F	G	L
L	X	D	R	U	I	D	M	E	Q
G	O	T	E	M	P	L	E	L	G
I	E	Y	R	T	N	A	F	N	I

2 a) What do you think this picture shows? Is it: (i) inside Stonehenge; (ii) inside Maiden Castle; (iii) inside Grime's Graves?
b) What was done here?
c) At which period in history was it used and why was it so important?

3 This book began in the years before Jesus Christ was born (BC). You have now reached the Roman period, after Christ's birth (AD). You need to be clear about dates and centuries so try to answer these questions:
a) In which century do these dates come: 55 BC; AD 43; AD 122; 376 BC.
b) Write down *any* one year from each of these centuries: 2nd century AD; 5th century BC; 1st century BC; 1st century AD.

4 Below are outline pictures of five people whom you have read about so far. Using the clues, write down the names of each of them.

REBEL QUEEN OF THE ICENI

ROMAN GENERAL WHO INVADED BRITAIN

EMPEROR WHO ORDERED A WALL TO BE BUILT

ROMAN LEADER WHO CONQUERED SOUTH-WEST ENGLAND

ROMAN EMPEROR WHO CONQUERED BRITAIN

15 Out Shopping . . .

A town street in Roman Britain – but don't believe everything you see! The artist has included some deliberate mistakes. (See question 4.)

There are no written accounts of what life was like in a town in Roman Britain. But archaeologists have studied the remains of Roman towns. Also, we know what life was like elsewhere in the Roman Empire.

The best shops were in the heart of town around the forum. But there were plenty of other shops in the streets nearby. Often, shops selling a particular item were close together. Sometimes, there would be a whole street of shops, each selling the same goods.

Of course, there were no supermarkets. In fact, most shops were quite tiny. Some were just part of an ordinary house and the shopkeeper and his family lived in the rooms behind or above the shop.

Each morning, he would walk through his house and open up the shutters at the front to show he was open for business. The shop was little more than one long counter. People stood on the pavement and bought their goods.

Apart from food shops, there were shops selling manufactured goods. There were no factories such as we have today. So these goods were often made in the same building, usually in a workshop behind the shop itself. A few workshops, such as pottery, needed a lot of workers, but most did not.

Some goods were made to put on display ready for anyone who wanted to buy them. But most things were made to order. When a customer wanted a new pair of sandals, he would select the leather and choose the style he wanted. Then, he went away to let the shopkeeper get on with making them. Often, they would be ready within 24 hours.

Some shopkeepers employed workmen to help them; often, they were slaves. If you wanted to be sure you were buying good quality goods, you could watch the men at work.

The streets were always busy in daytime. We would think they were smelly and dusty and it was even worse on market day. Indeed, rich people usually only went shopping to buy expensive items. So many of the shoppers were slaves, out shopping for their masters or mistresses.

In many ways, these shops were very different from those of our modern towns. But they *were* shops! What is so special about that? The answer is simple – there was nothing like them for over 600 years after the Romans left.

Pictures of different Roman shops.

1. Divide your page into two columns, using a pencil and ruler. Write the heading *Roman Shops* over one column and put *Modern Shops* over the other. Now, using the text *and* the evidence, list the differences between Roman shops and modern shops. You should find at least six differences.
2. a) What sort of shop is shown in evidence A?
   b) What is each person doing?
   c) What is the object (see arrow) and what is it used for?
3. Three other shops are shown. Write down the letters B, C and D. Beside each, write down what sort of shop it is.
4. Look at the scene on page 36. The artist has drawn a Roman street scene but he has included ten mistakes. Try to find all ten! Write down each one and explain why it is a mistake.
5. Imagine you are a slave sent out to do some shopping for your master. Describe what happens to you and what the streets and shops are like. Be sure not to make any mistakes like the artist did!

16 . . . and Back at Home

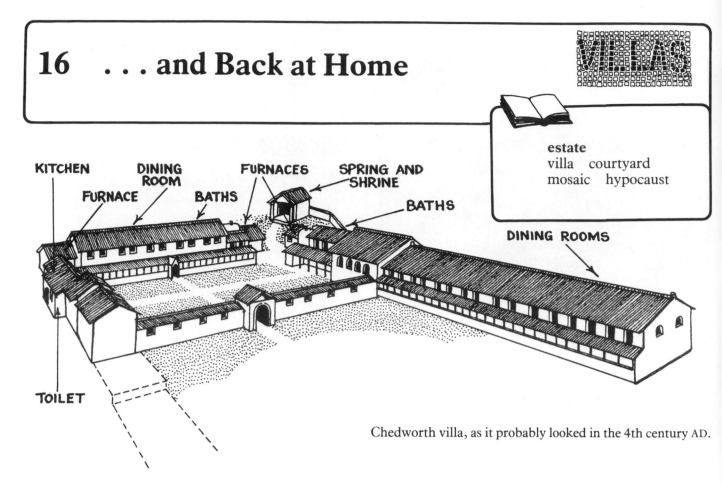

KITCHEN DINING ROOM FURNACES SPRING AND SHRINE

FURNACE BATHS BATHS

estate
villa courtyard
mosaic hypocaust

DINING ROOMS

TOILET

Chedworth villa, as it probably looked in the 4th century AD.

Despite the towns, nine out of ten people still lived in the countryside. Most Britons carried on living in huts, like those used before the Romans came. But rich Romans and Britons wanted something better. They chose to live in large homes on country **estates**, called villas.

Archaeologists have found the remains of over 600 of these, mostly in southern England. Many were found by chance, such as the fine villa at Chedworth in Gloucestershire. The picture above shows what it once looked like.

These villas were usually built in the valleys. Their owners made a living by farming the land around the villa. A few villas were quite small, no bigger than a modern house. Others were huge, such as the Palace at Fishbourne in Sussex, which had 80 rooms.

Chedworth villa was begun in the 2nd century AD but it was extended in the 4th century to look as it does in the picture. Like many other villas, it was built around a courtyard. The rooms were linked by corridors.

It could not have been more different from the houses which the Britons lived in before the Romans came. Walls were painted and floors had beautiful mosaic pictures on them. The mosaics

were made by laying thousands of small pieces of coloured stone on wet cement. But there was another, greater luxury which the Romans had invented. It was central heating.

It was a very simple system. The diagram below shows how it worked. The villa's heated rooms were built over a pit and a concrete floor was laid on pillars (A). Outside the room was space for a fire (B), made from charcoal.

A Roman central heating system. The space under the floor was called a hypocaust.

A This Roman living room has been made by a museum.

When the fire was lit, it heated the air under the rooms (C) and the warm air passed through the house and up hollow tiles into the walls of the rooms (D).

But the luxury did not end there. Roman villas also had their own bathrooms and sometimes a lavatory which flushed. And the windows were not just holes in the wall – they actually had glass in them!

Of course, a large villa meant a lot of housework. Yet there were no vacuum cleaners or washing machines; no gas cookers or dishwashers; none of the gadgets we have today.

How did the Roman housewife cope? She used something else. She used slaves – and lots of them.

1 Match up the words on the left with the correct meaning from the right:

mosaic	space under floors for hot air heating
hypocaust	space enclosed by walls
villa	small pieces of stone laid to form a picture or pattern
courtyard	a Roman country house

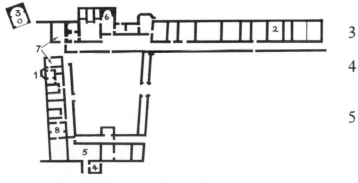

2 a) This is a plan of Chedworth villa. Draw it in your book. Make it larger than it is here.
b) Name each of the places shown by a number. Use the picture on page 38 to find the answers. For instance, 4 is the lavatory.
3 Write down four luxuries which a villa had which Iron Age houses had not had.
4 a) Draw the picture of the hypocaust.
b) Add your own captions to explain what happens at each place where there is a letter.
5 Look at evidence A. Write down the numbers 1 to 5 on separate lines in your book. Work out what each object is and write it beside the correct number.

17 A Slave's Life

There were slaves in Roman times, just as there had been in the Iron Age. Indeed, the Roman way of life *needed* slaves. It just would not have occurred to a rich Roman that you could live without them.

Most slaves had been captured in wars. While the Romans were still conquering, there was no shortage of them. But there were other sources of slaves, such as young children who had been abandoned. Fathers were even allowed to sell older children if they needed money.

A Roman who wanted to buy a slave could find people on sale in the market place. The price varied greatly. People with a trade cost more than most other slaves; good cooks could work out very expensive.

Once they were bought, slaves became slaves for life. Their only way out was to be set free by their master or to buy their freedom. Slaves paid the same price for their freedom as their master had paid when he bought them. It could take years to save up that kind of money.

A slave's children were slaves from the moment they were born. Slaves often killed their children rather than let this happen. At one British villa, the skeletons of 97 baby girls were found. They were probably slaves' babies, left outside to die.

We do not know exactly how many slaves there were in Roman Britain. In Rome itself, the number was huge. In later days, one person in four was a slave. The Emperor owned up to 20 000 and even a fairly well-off person had 500 or more.

Even in Britain, there must have been many slaves. They were needed in the mines and they did much of the farm work for villa owners; they were used by shopkeepers.

The sort of life they led depended on who owned them. Conditions in the mines were grim. But in a villa or on a farm, a fair master could make sure that a slave's life was not too awful. By the end of Roman times, slaves were in short supply. It was worth a master's while to look after his slaves. He might find it expensive to replace them.

A In the 1st century AD, Seneca wrote what he thought about slaves:

I'm glad to hear that you live on friendly terms with your slaves. It is just what one expects of someone like you. 'They're slaves,' people say. No. They're human beings. 'They're slaves.' But they share the same roof as ourselves. 'They're slaves.' No, they're friends. Strictly speaking, they're our fellow-slaves, because fate has as much power over us as over them.

That's why I laugh at those people who think it degrading for a man to eat with his slave. After all, it's only a custom that the master of the house should be surrounded at dinner by a crowd of slaves, who have to stand around while he eats more than he can hold. [They watch him] loading up his swollen belly until it cannot do its job any more.

Then, he uses more effort to vomit everything up than he did to force it down. And all this time the poor slaves are forbidden to speak, let alone to eat. The slightest murmur is checked with a stick. Even a cough or hiccup earns him a beating.

The result is that slaves who cannot talk before his face talk about him behind his back. It is this sort of treatment which makes people say, 'You've as many enemies as you've slaves.' They are not our enemies when we get them; we make them so.

B Slaves help their mistress.

THE SLAVES' DAY IN A ROMAN VILLA

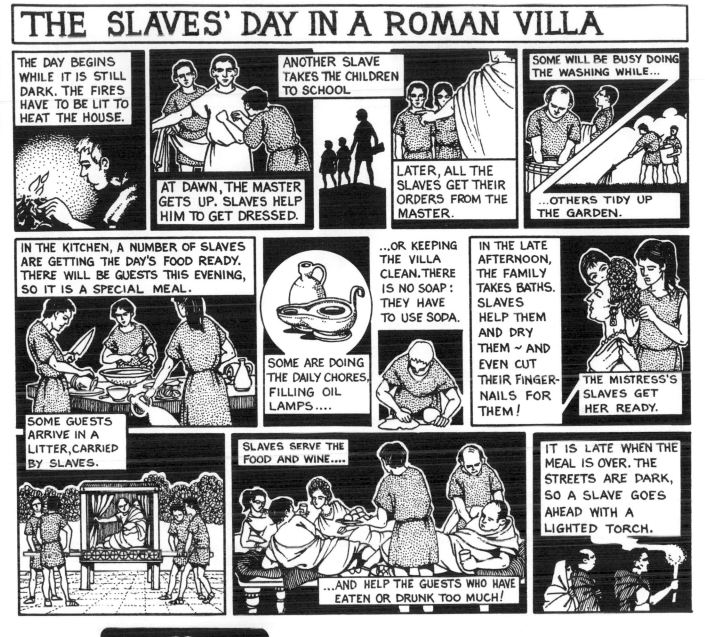

THE DAY BEGINS WHILE IT IS STILL DARK. THE FIRES HAVE TO BE LIT TO HEAT THE HOUSE.

AT DAWN, THE MASTER GETS UP. SLAVES HELP HIM TO GET DRESSED.

ANOTHER SLAVE TAKES THE CHILDREN TO SCHOOL

LATER, ALL THE SLAVES GET THEIR ORDERS FROM THE MASTER.

SOME WILL BE BUSY DOING THE WASHING WHILE...

...OTHERS TIDY UP THE GARDEN.

IN THE KITCHEN, A NUMBER OF SLAVES ARE GETTING THE DAY'S FOOD READY. THERE WILL BE GUESTS THIS EVENING, SO IT IS A SPECIAL MEAL.

SOME ARE DOING THE DAILY CHORES, FILLING OIL LAMPS....

...OR KEEPING THE VILLA CLEAN. THERE IS NO SOAP: THEY HAVE TO USE SODA.

IN THE LATE AFTERNOON, THE FAMILY TAKES BATHS. SLAVES HELP THEM AND DRY THEM ~ AND EVEN CUT THEIR FINGER-NAILS FOR THEM!

THE MISTRESS'S SLAVES GET HER READY.

SOME GUESTS ARRIVE IN A LITTER, CARRIED BY SLAVES.

SLAVES SERVE THE FOOD AND WINE....

...AND HELP THE GUESTS WHO HAVE EATEN OR DRUNK TOO MUCH!

IT IS LATE WHEN THE MEAL IS OVER. THE STREETS ARE DARK, SO A SLAVE GOES AHEAD WITH A LIGHTED TORCH.

1 Answer these questions in full sentences:
   a) What sorts of people became slaves?
   b) Where did you go to buy slaves?
   c) How could a slave become free?
   d) Where did slaves work?
2 Read evidence A.
   a) Divide your page into two columns with a pencil line. In the two columns, write the reasons for and against having slaves.
   b) What do you think are the main reasons why people today think slavery is wrong?
3 If *you* had been a slave and had a child, would you have killed it? Explain your decision in detail.
4 Look at the strip cartoon above.
   a) Imagine you are one of the slaves. A new slave has come to your house and you have to explain the duties to him or her. Write down what you would say.
   b) Draw two other scenes from a slave's day. Look at pages 38 and 39 for ideas.

18 Going to School

WRITING AT SECONDARY SCHOOL
INK MADE FROM SOOT
SCROLL MADE FROM PAPYRUS (REEDS)

abacus
stylus

It is a winter's morning and still dark. Boys and girls of seven upwards are making their way along the cold streets to school. Some carry burning torches to light their way; others are guided by a slave. One or two stop to buy a hot bun at the baker's.

YOU'RE LATE: IT'S VI PAST IX!

School lasts for about six hours, with no break until the pupils go home for lunch. Few of these children will spend the day in a school building. Many schools are held outside a shop, with just a curtain to separate the pupils from the busy street outside.

There are no desks, either. The children sit on benches or stools and hold wooden boards on their laps on which they write. Some of the pupils are nervous. They are worried that they have got their homework wrong. One or two are in a tearing hurry because they are late.

They have good reason to be nervous. The master is very strict and quick to use a cane to beat pupils who are not doing their best. Parents have to pay the masters to teach their children and they expect them to be firm.

Perhaps the teachers need to be harsh because lessons can get very dull. The seven-year-olds spend their time learning the names of the Latin letters. They simply say them over and over again until they know them. Then, they learn how to write them by copying them regularly.

There are no books to help them. The teacher dictates words, letter by letter, and the children learn them by heart. Later, they will repeat it to the teacher: if they get anything wrong, they will be beaten.

The other main subject is arithmetic, often taught by another master. They have to learn much of this by heart, too, although there may be an **abacus** to help them. Even so, they start by spending a long time counting up on their fingers.

The pupils leave primary school at 11 or 12. The girls might carry on their lessons at home, although they can get married when they are 12. (Boys have to wait until they are 14!) That leaves the boys to go on to secondary school on their own.

There, they carry on learning Latin, Greek and arithmetic, but there are also new subjects. They need to know history and geography in order to understand Roman writers. And they also learn about the stars.

Above all, they learn to speak in public. Giving lectures is an important part of growing up.

In early Roman times, there were no games on the timetable. Even music was only added later, along with dancing. However, pupils left school early in the afternoon so they could enjoy games then.

What else was missing? Weekends were missing! Roman children worked a seven-day week. The eighth day was market day and schools were closed. They also closed for religious festivals and most pupils had summer holidays. Apart from that, *every* day was a school day!

A Writing was done in wax on a wooden tablet. People wrote with a stylus (shown in the picture) or just with a stick. The wax could be smoothed over and used again and again.

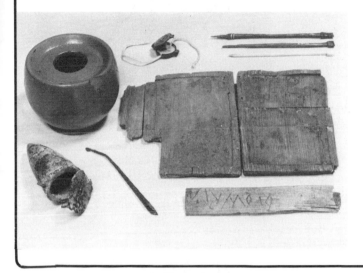

B Quintilian gave his views on teaching in the 1st century AD:

The skilful teacher will make it his first task to discover how able his pupil is and what his character is like. My ideal pupil will easily cope with instruction and will even ask some questions; but he will follow his teacher rather than try to get ahead of him.

The teacher must next decide how to deal with his pupil. Some boys are lazy, unless forced to work; others do not like being controlled; some will respond to fear but others are paralysed by it. Give me a boy who is encouraged by praise, delighted by success and ready to weep over failure. Such a boy must be encouraged by appeals to his ambition.

Still, all our pupils need some relaxation because study depends on a student's good will and you cannot force him to give you that. If refreshed by a holiday, they will bring more energy to their work and come to it with greater spirit. A boy who is gloomy and always depressed is never likely to show a lively mind in his work.

Rich people paid tutors to teach their children at home. One tutor had a bright idea to make reading easier. He wrote the Latin letters on big posters and got 24 slaves to carry them round!

1 a) Copy out this paragraph filling in the gaps:
   Many Roman schools were held outside a
   _____ . The youngest children began by
   learning the names of the _____ letters. They
   learnt these by _____ . For arithmetic, they
   had an _____ to help them.
   b) Which subjects did they study which you do
   not?

2 a) Write down, in sentences, *at least* five differences between a Roman primary school and the one you went to.
   b) What would you have liked *and* disliked most about a Roman school? Why?

3 Make an outline sketch of the objects shown in evidence A. On your sketch, name each object from this list: inkwell; stylus; pens; seal-box to hold wax; wooden tablet.

4 Read evidence B. Write down all those things he said with which you agree and all those with which you disagree.

sewer drug
amputated
theriac trepanning

Nobody understood better than the Romans the need for public health. Towns were supplied with fresh water and drinking basins were set up in the streets. Rich people had lead pipes in their houses so that they did not have to go and fetch water. Many of them even had baths.

Towns such as Bath and York had a system of **sewers** which were also linked to public lavatories. Even on Hadrian's Wall, the lavatories had running water.

The Romans realised that they needed trained doctors if people were to stay healthy. Many Roman towns had doctors who looked after the townspeople; the army had its own doctors to keep the troops fit; even the schools where men learned to become gladiators had their own doctors. They needed them!

Medicine had some strange ingredients!

Eye trouble seems to have been common in Roman Britain. All these medicines were on sale.

The first doctors in Rome had come from Greece and people had been suspicious of them. One politician even thought that they had come to murder the Romans! But the Greek doctors soon showed that they knew their job. Roman doctors later owed much of their skill to the Greeks. No one was to improve on this for well over 1000 years.

Even so, there was little guarantee that they could make people better. Doctors often gave their patients lots of **drugs** at once, in the hope that one of them would work.

Most drugs were made out of herbs and other plants. Cucumber seeds were supposed to be good for fever and nettle tea was given for rheumatism. One special drug, called theriac, was used to deal with poisoning; amongst other things, it included snake flesh.

But the doctors' cures were better than the medicine which could be bought from a travelling salesman on market day. All sorts of creams and liquids were on sale and the salesman promised that they would cure just about anything. In fact, they were nearly all useless!

A Medical instruments used by Roman doctors. They include spatulas (A and B), spatula with probe (C), retractor for holding down the tongue (D), saw for sawing bones (E), forceps for holding or removing something, probably an artery (F).

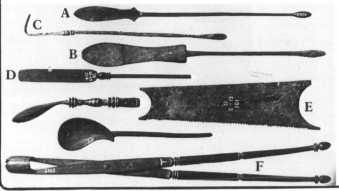

Even so, there was no shortage of work for genuine doctors. The army needed hospitals for wounded soldiers and, later, there were hospitals for the poor and even one for slaves. Some hospitals had operating theatres where even dangerous operations were carried out.

The doctors used drugs made from herbs to send a patient to sleep while they operated on the head, removed tonsils or even **amputated** arms and legs. Some doctors could provide false limbs for the patient to wear afterwards.

After the end of the Roman Empire, much of this knowledge was lost. Christians often thought that disease was sent by God to punish the wicked. So the sick turned to prayers, rather than doctors.

But one thing did not change. The Church continued to look after the sick, even if it often could not make them better.

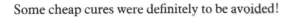
Some cheap cures were definitely to be avoided!

B One operation which was carried out was trepanning. It involved boring a hole in the skull to remove pressure from the brain, either to treat an injury or to deal with a nervous illness. This skull was found at Rockbourne Villa in Hampshire.

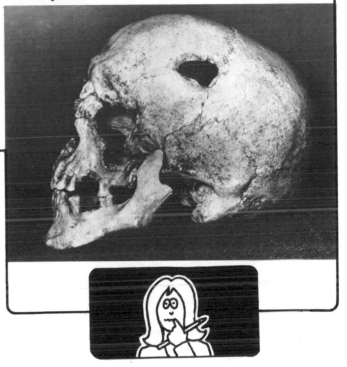

1 Write one sentence to explain each of these words: drug; rheumatism; theriac; operating theatre; trepanning; amputate.
2 The Romans improved public health in various ways. Write down each of the following and explain how it would help: pure drinking water; proper sewers; trained doctors; hospitals; anaesthetics made from herbs.
3 a) Draw the medical instruments (evidence A). b) Beside each one, write what you think it was used for. Use the caption to help you.
4 a) Why do you think the Romans had been suspicious of Greek doctors? b) Why did the Christians think prayer would make people better?
5 What modern equipment did Roman doctors *not* have to help them cure people? You should think of at least six things. Use your library, if necessary.
6 People said that in Rome the rich got sick from eating, while the poor got sick from not eating. What do you think they meant?

20 Bath

One road which the Romans built was the Fosse Way. As it heads west, it crosses the River Avon and nearby the Romans found something unique in Britain: hot springs. Every day, over a million litres of water came up to the surface at a temperature of about 48°C. It still does today. We call the place Bath.

The Romans were delighted. They loved bathing. Most Roman towns had public baths and Rome itself eventually had nearly a thousand. It cost next to nothing to get in and rich Romans tried to go every day. It was part of their way of life.

The Romans did not go to the baths just to get clean, although that was important. The baths were more like a club: they met their friends and played games, as well as going swimming and bathing. There were separate baths for the different sexes at Bath.

The first job the Romans had to do was to control the springs. The **reservoir** they built was so good that it is still there today. Around it, they added the baths and a temple and, soon, a town.

The Romans thought that the spring was **sacred** so they went there to ask for special favours from the gods. Many of them threw valuable objects, such as coins and jewellery, into the spring as gifts to the gods. Someone even threw in a piece of lead, with a curse written on it backwards so that only the gods could read it.

Nearby, the Romans built an **altar** where a priest sacrificed animals to the gods. The animals were also cut open and people looked at the insides to help them predict the future.

The Romans believed that the hot water could heal the sick so people came to Bath from all over the Empire to get better. Not all of them did. Roman tombstones from Bath show that, while a few people lived long lives, the average age of death was just 38. People were lucky to live beyond 45.

A Seneca described a bath in Rome:

Just imagine every kind of annoying noise! The sturdy gentleman does his exercises with lead weights; when he is working hard (or pretending to) I can hear him grunt; when he breathes out, I can hear him panting in high-pitched tones.

Or I might notice some lazy fellow, content with a cheap rub-down, and hear the blows of the hand slapping his shoulders. The sound varies, depending on whether the **massager** hits with a flat or hollow hand.

To all this, you can add the arrest of the occasional pickpocket; there's also the racket made by the man who loves to hear his own voice in the bath or the chap who dives in with a lot of noise and splashing.

On top of all this, there's the hair-plucker shouting out in a shrill voice to catch attention. The only time he keeps quiet is when he is plucking hairs out of someone's armpits and making *them* cry instead.

B The Great Bath in the baths at Bath!

MARCUS GOES TO THE BATHS.

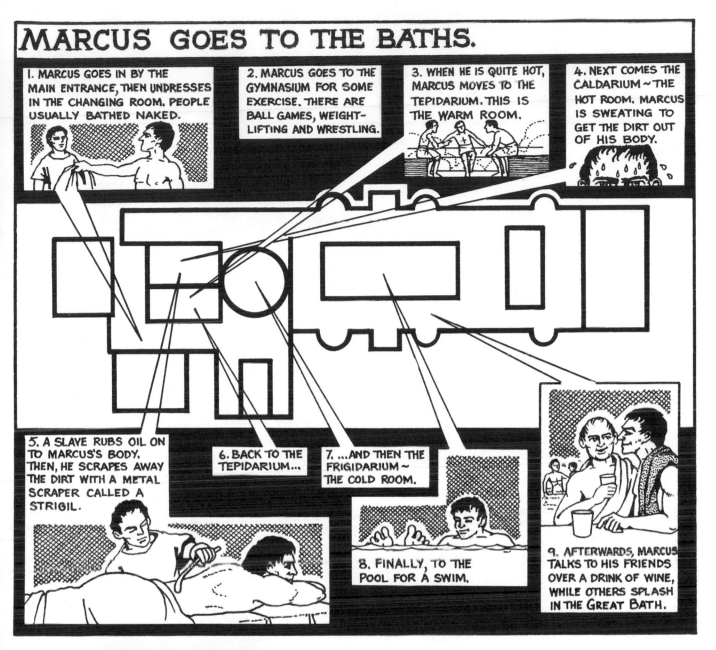

1. MARCUS GOES IN BY THE MAIN ENTRANCE, THEN UNDRESSES IN THE CHANGING ROOM. PEOPLE USUALLY BATHED NAKED.

2. MARCUS GOES TO THE GYMNASIUM FOR SOME EXERCISE. THERE ARE BALL GAMES, WEIGHT-LIFTING AND WRESTLING.

3. WHEN HE IS QUITE HOT, MARCUS MOVES TO THE TEPIDARIUM. THIS IS THE WARM ROOM.

4. NEXT COMES THE CALDARIUM ~ THE HOT ROOM. MARCUS IS SWEATING TO GET THE DIRT OUT OF HIS BODY.

5. A SLAVE RUBS OIL ON TO MARCUS'S BODY. THEN, HE SCRAPES AWAY THE DIRT WITH A METAL SCRAPER CALLED A STRIGIL.

6. BACK TO THE TEPIDARIUM...

7. ...AND THEN THE FRIGIDARIUM ~ THE COLD ROOM.

8. FINALLY, TO THE POOL FOR A SWIM.

9. AFTERWARDS, MARCUS TALKS TO HIS FRIENDS OVER A DRINK OF WINE, WHILE OTHERS SPLASH IN THE GREAT BATH.

1 Answer these questions in full sentences:
  a) What was special about the Bath spring?
  b) What was the Romans' first task at Bath?
  c) Why did they build a temple nearby?
  d) For what reasons did the Romans sacrifice animals?
  e) What else could the Romans do at the baths, apart from get clean?
2 a) Draw the plan of the baths shown above.
  b) Read the text and mark on your plan the route you would have taken through the baths.
3 Describe a visit to the baths with your mother or father. Use the pictures and evidence to give as much detail as possible.
4 a) How do people try to predict the future nowadays?
  b) Do you think that it is a better way than cutting up animals? Explain your answer.
5 Imagine you wanted to make a curse on someone. Write your curse backwards and don't be too cruel! Try it out on rough paper first – writing backwards isn't easy!

21 Roman Amusements

stadium   amphitheatre
charioteer

The remains of the Colosseum today.

One of the most famous sights in Rome today is the ruins of the Colosseum. It was once a huge **stadium**, built to hold over 50 000 people. The audience was shielded from the sun by a big cover which roared like thunder when the wind was strong.

Below ground there was another kind of roaring. It came from the wild animals which were caged up, ready to be brought to the surface. They were there to amuse the crowd.

Some would do circus tricks; most were there to fight. Bears fought buffaloes and buffaloes fought elephants or, instead, all of them were hunted by men. Some types of animal died out in parts of the Roman Empire – just to amuse the crowds. On just one day, when the Colosseum opened, 5000 animals died.

But the crowds really came to see people, not animals, being killed. The main part of the show was the fights of the gladiators. Most of them were slaves or prisoners-of-war; others were so poor that fighting to death seemed better than starving to death.

Marching past the Emperor, they cried, 'Hail, Emperor, those who are about to die salute thee!' Probably half of them would be dead before the day was out.

Organisers usually tried to arrange as many different kinds of contest as possible, to give the crowd more fun. Just occasionally, two gladiators fought to a draw; but usually, one of them was killed. Sometimes, one simply could not go on fighting and laid down his arms.

It was the Emperor's job to decide whether the gladiator lived or died. If he had fought well, the Emperor might give the 'thumbs up' sign, which meant that he should live; the 'thumbs down' sign allowed the winner to kill the loser. If the Emperor was not present, the winner decided whether to kill his opponent or not.

Nothing as big as the Colosseum was ever built in Britain, but there were **amphitheatres** at towns such as Cirencester. Gladiators may have fought there, like at the Colosseum.

Another great Roman entertainment existed in Britain. This was the theatre. By the 4th century AD, the Romans had over 100 days' holiday a year just to go to the theatre. There, they watched plays or concerts or listened to poetry.

THE RETIARIUS FOUGHT WITH TRIDENT AND NET. THE SECUTOR FOUGHT WITH SHIELD AND SWORD.

ONE SLIP WAS THE DIFFERENCE BETWEEN LIFE AND DEATH.

AFTERWARDS, THEY CHECKED TO SEE IF THE LOSER WAS DEAD BY HITTING HIS FOREHEAD WITH A MALLET.

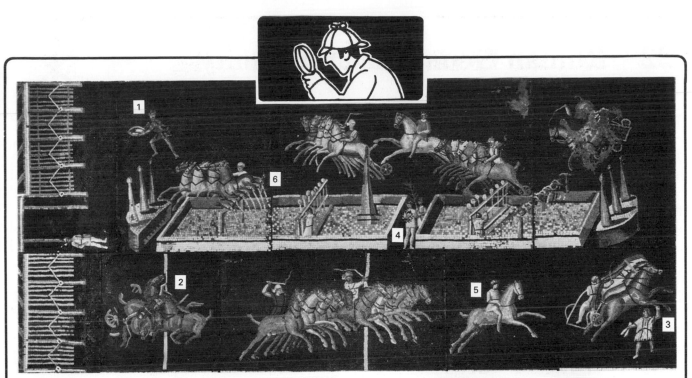

A Chariot-racing at the circus was also popular. Driving a four-horse chariot needed skill and daring, and the best charioteers were as popular as modern pop stars. However, even the best often died in their early 20s.

B Seneca described another kind of contest – between criminals. Their punishment was to die fighting.

I happened to go to one of these shows at the lunch-hour interval, expecting to find an amusing entertainment as a rest from seeing human blood. Far from it. What [I saw] is murder, pure and simple. The fighters have nothing to protect them; their whole bodies are exposed and every thrust gets home. A great many spectators prefer this to the ordinary matches.

And quite naturally. There are no helmets or shields. What is the point of armour? It just makes death slower in coming. In the morning, men are thrown to the lions and the bears. But in the lunch hour they are thrown to the spectators.

The spectators insist that, as soon as one has killed a man, he fights someone else so that, in turn, he too is killed. The final winner will be reserved for some other form of death. The only exit is death.

When there is an interval in the show, [someone shouts]: 'Let's have some throats cut in the meantime so that there's something happening!' Surely you people realise that setting a bad example can spring back on you? Give thanks to the gods that the men to whom you are giving a lesson in cruelty are not able to benefit from it.

1 Write one sentence about each of the words in the word box.
2 Which of these words do you think describe gladiator fights: cruel; amusing; fair; popular; vicious; exciting; wrong. For each word you choose, give reasons for it.
3 a) Describe a contest between a retiarius and a secutor, as if you were watching it.
   b) Draw a scene from the contest.
4 Look at evidence A above. Write the numbers 1 to 6 on separate lines of your book. Now, pick out these people and events and match them with the right number: a) an official whipping the horses on; b) a single horseman, probably setting the pace; c) the figures used to show the number of laps; d) a man throwing water on the chariot wheels; e) a chariot which has had an accident; f) officials ready with the winner's wreath.
5 a) Read and discuss evidence B. Do you think this was a fair way to punish criminals?
   b) Do you agree with what Seneca thought?
6 Draw a poster to announce a special day at the arena, with gladiators and wild beasts.

22 Roman Gods and Christianity

There was another way of killing criminals in the arena. It was simple and it was brutal. At dawn, they were dragged into the arena and wild beasts were let loose upon them, mauling them to death. It was a punishment which the Romans often used against Christians.

There were Christians in Rome by AD 50 and the Roman emperors did their best to get rid of them. The Christians, they thought, were a threat. After all, the Romans had their own gods.

One of these gods was the Emperor himself. The Romans built a temple to the Emperor Claudius at Colchester and the British hated it. There were heavy taxes to pay for the services held there. When Boudica attacked the town in AD 60, one of the things her followers did was to wreck it.

There were temples to other gods, too. The most powerful was Jupiter, chief of the gods, but there was also Juno, goddess of women, and Minerva, goddess of wisdom, amongst others. The temples were small, so important **ceremonies** took place outside. In front, an altar was set up where animals could be sacrificed.

Soldiers helped to spread the worship of gods from other parts of the Empire. One of these was Mithras. He was supposed to have sacrificed a sacred bull to defeat the forces of evil. The sacrifice was in a cave, so his temples had no windows and were often built partly underground, to look like a cave.

Blazing torches provided light while the worshippers ate a sacred meal, lying on benches along the walls. They had to take various tests if they wanted to reach the highest rank in the faith.

But, from the East came a new religion to rival all these. It was Christianity. In place of all the Roman gods, it offered just one God. Instead of sacrifices, it offered **baptism** by pure water. Instead of stories from ancient **myths**, it offered the example of Jesus, God's son. Above all, it spoke of love.

Earlier emperors had thrown Christians to the lions; later ones became Christian themselves. In AD 391 worship of other gods was banned in the Roman Empire. It must have seemed to British Christians that they were safe, at last.

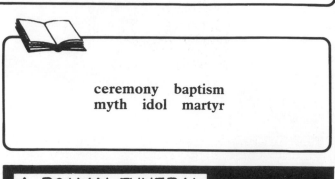

ceremony   baptism
myth   idol   martyr

A ROMAN FUNERAL

A coin was put into the dead person's mouth. People thought that a boatman would row the soul across the river of the dead. The coin was his payment.

The body was carried out of the town on a couch. People were paid to cry and wail as they went along. It made sure that the dead person's spirit knew how sad everyone was. Otherwise, it might return to haunt them.

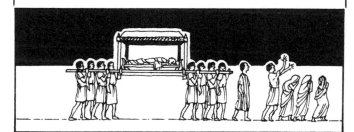

The body was laid on a funeral fire to be cremated. The ashes were put in a pot called an urn, which was buried. Sometimes, personal possessions were buried, too. Romans thought that the spirit might need these in the next world.

It was not so. Far away, in Rome itself, the Empire was under threat. It would not be long before the Romans' problems would put British Christians at risk too.

A In AD 731, a monk called Bede described how one Christian called Alban was killed. Alban had only recently become a Christian and, to save a priest, he dressed up as the priest and was arrested. He was taken before a judge who, at that moment, was making a sacrifice. (Bede said it happened in AD 301, although it was probably 50 years earlier.)

'Since you have chosen to conceal a rebel,' he said, 'rather than surrender him to my soldiers, you shall undergo all the tortures due to him if you dare to abandon the practice of our religion.'
   But St Alban refused to obey this order. He replied, 'If you wish to know the truth about my religion, I am a Christian, and I worship and adore the true God, who created all things.'
   The judge was very angry, and said, 'If you want to enjoy everlasting life, sacrifice at once to the great gods.'
   Alban replied: 'You are offering these sacrifices to devils and whoever offers sacrifices to **idols** is doomed to the pains of hell.'
   Made even angrier, the judge ordered Alban to be flogged, hoping to change his mind by torture. But, for Christ's sake, he put up with the most horrible pains, so the judge ordered Alban to be beheaded.
   Led outside, the saint came to a river which flowed between the town wall and the arena where he was to die. Such a huge crowd had gathered that he could hardly have crossed. Saint Alban wished for a quick death and, as he raised his eyes to heaven in prayer, the river ran dry in its bed and left him a way to cross.
   When the executioner saw this, he was so moved that he threw down his sword and fell at Alban's feet, begging to die with the **martyr** if he could not die in his place.
   Meanwhile, Alban walked up the hill, accompanied by the crowd. As he reached the top, holy Alban asked God to give him water and at once a stream bubbled up at his feet. Here, the brave martyr met his death. But the man who killed him was not allowed to boast of his deed because, when Alban's head fell, his eyes dropped out on to the ground.

B Part of a 4th century mosaic from Dorset. The picture is probably of Christ. Behind him is a secret symbol used by Christians and made up of the letters Chi (χ) and Rho (ρ) – the first two letters of Christ's name in Greek.

1 Match up the words on the left with the correct description from the right:

martyr   god worshipped by Romans
Mithras   person who dies for a belief
AD 391   chief of the Roman gods
Jupiter   worship of all other gods banned

2 a) In your own words describe a Roman funeral.
   b) How is it different from a modern funeral?
   c) Draw a scene from a Roman funeral. (Don't just copy one!)

3 Look at evidence B. Imagine you were a Christian when Christians were still being hunted down. Design a mosaic which will prove to other Christians that you are a Christian, without making it too obvious.

4 a) Read evidence A. How long after Alban's death did Bede write about it?
   b) How might Bede have found out about it after all that time?
   c) Was Bede biased for or against Alban? Give examples to support your decision.
   d) Is there anything you do not believe about this story? If so, write down what it is and say why you do not believe it.

barbarian

The Romans ruled Britain for over 350 years. For more than half this time, it was peaceful and many Britons enjoyed the Roman way of life. There were luxuries from all over the Empire and new cities to buy them in. It must have seemed to many Britons as if it would go on for ever. They were wrong.

From AD 250 onwards, the Romans began to have problems keeping Britain safe. Despite Hadrian's Wall, the Picts carried out raids; so did the Scots, who lived in Ireland. Worst of all were the Angles and Saxons who came from across the North Sea to destroy and steal.

The Romans built huge forts along the south and east coasts but still the raiders came.

In any case, the Romans had other problems on their minds. Their Empire was huge: it needed an army of at least 500 000 men to guard it. By the end of the 4th century, over half of the soldiers were **barbarians**, not Romans.

Meanwhile, outside the Empire, other barbarians from northern Europe looked hungrily in. Rome was wealthy: they wanted a share in it. The Roman Empire was vast: they wanted land.

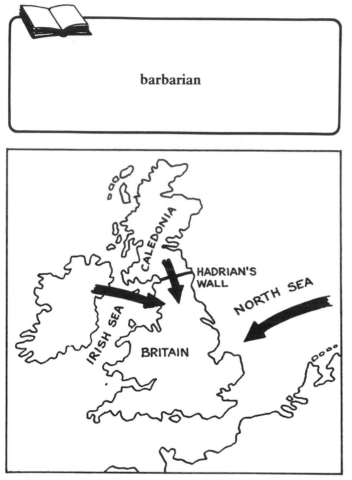

Britain was under attack from all sides.

The Roman North Sea Fleet went to great lengths to camouflage itself. Ships had blue sails and ropes, while sailors dressed in blue uniforms.

ROMANS HIRED BARBARIAN SOLDIERS TO FIGHT OTHER BARBARIANS

TOO MANY UNEMPLOYED

THE RICH HAD GROWN LAZY

There were many things wrong in Rome itself.

As time passed, more and more soldiers from far corners of the Empire were called home to help keep these attackers out. Britain was right at the edge of the Roman Empire and, from AD 300, soldiers were being taken away. Life became more dangerous so the rich stayed in their country villas. The towns began to crumble.

It was the troubles elsewhere which finally ended Roman rule in Britain. One cold night, in December AD 406, 15 000 barbarians walked across the frozen River Rhine into Gaul. There was hardly anyone to stop them.

In the following year, the army in Britain chose a new leader, called Constantine. He was just an ordinary soldier and he wanted to make a name for himself. So he set out for Gaul, taking the last of the Roman troops with him.

But the Britons still thought they were part of the Roman Empire. When they wanted help, they sent a message to Emperor Honorius in Rome. His reply was blunt: the Britons must learn to look after themselves.

The Emperor had no choice. The year was AD 410 and, in that year, Rome itself was attacked. No one defended it. People simply fled to the hills.

The Britons, however, did not give up. In about AD 446, they sent one last, desperate letter:

> To Aetius, three times Consul, come the groans of the Britons. The barbarians drive us into the sea, and the sea drives us back to the barbarians. Between them, we are faced with two deadly choices: either we are drowned or we are killed.

This time, they didn't even get a reply.

1 Below are some reasons why the Roman Empire collapsed. Some are right and some are wrong. Write out the correct ones.
   a) The Empire was too big to defend easily.
   b) The people had supported the enemy.
   c) No one wanted to become Emperor.
   d) Barbarians wanted to gain land.
2 a) Draw the map on page 52.
   b) On it, name the three groups of people who were attacking Britain.
3 Imagine you were writing a letter to the Emperor, asking for help to defend Britain. You will need to persuade him better than the Britons did in AD 410! Write your letter, giving reasons why he should help.
4 The square below contains the names of some towns in Roman Britain. Find as many as you can, using this book. Use your library to find others and, for each town, write down what the Romans called it.

B	R	U	E	X	E	T	E	R	T
A	Z	P	R	A	A	L	C	D	R
Y	W	R	E	T	S	I	A	C	D
O	R	H	T	L	O	N	M	D	F
R	E	T	S	E	H	C	L	O	C
K	W	A	E	H	C	O	M	V	K
I	C	B	H	L	N	L	J	E	Y
F	Y	V	C	D	E	N	I	R	M
K	B	G	O	Y	G	F	A	L	V
R	S	N	A	B	L	A	T	S	H

The Anglo-Saxons had many reasons for settling in Britain.

No one is really sure about much of what happened in Britain over the next 200 years. Most of the people who wrote about this period were writing after it was over and we cannot be sure where they got their facts from. But we do know that one sight would have been very common for many Britons.

They soon became used to seeing, in the springtime, grey-green boats with leather sails heading across the North Sea towards their land.

They were not large boats. Most were probably about 3 metres across and just over 20 metres long. Each one carried about 40 people.

Where the new invaders came from.

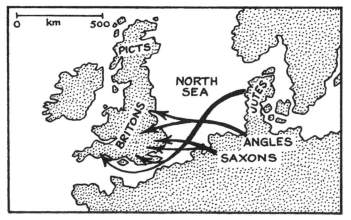

These people were from Europe; many of them were from tribes called Angles and Saxons. They had come in Roman times to raid. Now, they were coming to conquer and stay.

The Romans had looked down on them as savages: they called them barbarians. They were fierce and brutal fighters, but no worse than the Romans could be. When they came to Britain, they could not read or write but, in the centuries which followed, they were to produce fine poems and beautiful works of art.

And they were very determined. Their little boats brought across over 100 000 people. For about 150 years, they rowed across the North Sea, bringing settlers. When they arrived in Britain, they rowed up the rivers looking for a good place to live.

The Roman towns, with their huge stone buildings, could have been suitable places. But the Anglo-Saxons were not town-dwellers. They were farming folk and thought that the Roman towns must have been built by giants.

So they usually rowed past and made their homes on rich farmland in the valleys, where they could grow their crops. Later, they might go back to the towns to collect stones to build their huts on.

Sometimes, the Britons put up a fight against the newcomers but the Anglo-Saxons were good warriors. Most of the time, they won, and the Britons were gradually pushed back to the west and north. By AD 650, the Anglo-Saxons controlled most of England. A new race of conquerors had come to stay.

A ship's figure-head from about AD 400.

1 Below are the names of four people mentioned in this chapter, but the letters have been muddled up. Write the name out correctly and explain what each person did.
RSHOA; GTHSENI; EEDB; VINTREGOR.

2 a) Draw the map on page 54.
b) Using an atlas, work out the modern names for the countries from which the invaders came.
c) Whereabouts in Britain could the Britons go to escape from the invaders?

3 Look at the top picture on page 54. Suppose you were a Saxon invader. List the five reasons for coming in order of their importance to you. For instance, if number 3 was your main reason, write that down first. Then, give reasons for your order.

4 a) Write down two reasons why the Romans thought the Saxons were barbarians.
b) Why did the Saxons settle in the valleys?

5 Look carefully at the ship's figure-head.
a) Why do you think it was made like this?
b) Draw a frightening figure-head of your own.

This story may explain why some Saxons came here. It was written down in the 8th century by Bede.

KING VORTIGERN AND THE SAXONS

1 AD 449. A British king called Vortigern is fighting the Picts. He asked some Saxons to come and help.

2 The Saxon leaders are called Hengist and Horsa. Vortigern promises them land in return for their aid.

3 After they defeat the Picts, more Saxons come. The Britons go on giving money and land in return for guarding the island.

4 Then, the Saxons changed sides and joined up with the Picts. They fought the Britons and captured all Kent. King Vortigern was driven out.

25 Saxon Villages

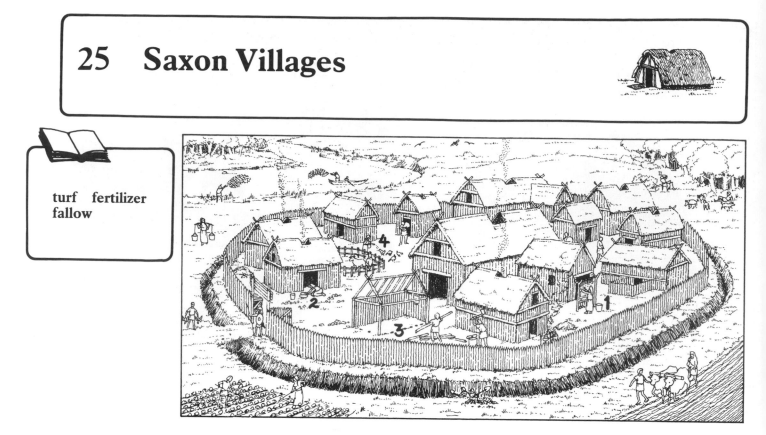

A Saxon village. The numbers are referred to in question 1.

Once they had chosen where to live, the Saxons' first job was to build homes for themselves. They cut down trees to make the framework and used **turf** or reeds for the roof. Sometimes, the walls were made of wattle and daub.

The more important people were, the bigger their homes would be. The very simplest homes were just huts built over pits in the ground. Others had walls made of split tree trunks. The village lord had a hall, which was the biggest building in the village.

Some Saxon chiefs eventually became kings. The main kingdoms are shown here. Northumbria was the most powerful in the 7th century but, by the 9th century, Wessex was the chief kingdom.

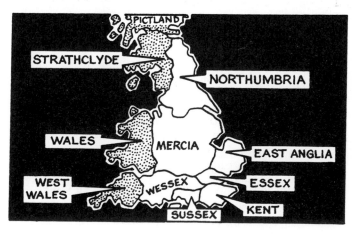

After building their homes, the villagers set about producing food. First, they had to clear some land for farming. The Britons had always farmed on the light soil of the hillsides but the Anglo-Saxons had a heavy plough, so they could farm in the valleys.

Two or three very big fields were made for growing crops such as barley and wheat. These fields were divided into strips. Each family had strips dotted around the fields, so everybody shared the good and bad land. In their own gardens, they grew vegetables, such as cabbages and onions.

Of course, the Saxons did not have all the **fertilizers** that a modern farmer uses. If they had just gone on growing crops on the same soil, year after year, the land would soon have lost its goodness.

So, each year, one of the big fields was not used. It lay **fallow** and the animals were allowed to graze on the grass which grew there. This added manure to the land, which improved the soil.

Many modern towns are still named after Saxon villages. If you find any of these endings in a modern name, it is likely that Saxons once lived there.

The Saxons did not have tractors, either. A team of oxen was used to pull the wooden plough which was used to till the soil. Sometimes, they just used spades tipped with iron instead. It would have been hard, back-breaking work.

Some of the villagers were known as 'freemen'. They owned or rented land from the lord. But most people were given land by the lord, on condition that they did some work on his land. The people who came off worst were the slaves. They had no land at all.

The Romans may have thought that the Saxons were barbarians, but they had worked out a way of life which gave them just about everything they needed. Just two things were missing – salt and iron. To get those, they would have to swap some of their spare food.

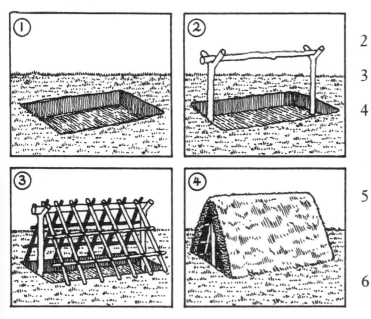

A step-by-step guide to building your own Saxon hut. It would have measured about 4 metres by 3 metres.

1 Draw or trace an outline picture of the Saxon village shown on page 56. Think carefully while you do this, so you are ready to answer these questions:
a) List all the useful items which the Saxons could get in or near their village. It was not all food. For instance, the sheep provided wool.
b) Next, list as many jobs as you can which needed doing regularly. The four numbers are clues to start you off, but you should come up with *at least* twelve jobs. See who can spot the most.

2 Why do you think the Saxons needed (a) salt and (b) iron?

3 Write one paragraph about how they organised their farming.

4 Look at the Saxon place names shown above. Using a modern atlas, try to find at least two places which include each of these words. If you live in England, start by looking in your own area.

5 a) How did the Saxons manage without (i) tractors and (ii) fertilizers?
b) What do you think they used instead of (i) sugar; (ii) drinking water; (iii) gas fires; (iv) chimneys; (v) ovens.

6 It would make an unusual class project if you actually built a Saxon hut! However, you can make one from twigs and straw. Build it on a papier-mâché base and keep it to scale.

26 King Arthur: Is it History or just a Story?

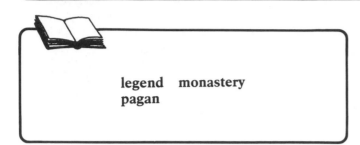

legend   monastery
pagan

One story has survived from those 200 years after the Romans left Britain. It tells of an amazing man who led the Britons. It was such a popular story that, by the 12th century, songs about him were being sung right across Europe.

Ever since, people have gone on writing or making films about him. His story became one of the world's great **legends**. He was King Arthur.

King Arthur became a major figure in history in the 12th century when a monk called Geoffrey gave him a whole chapter in his book about the Kings of Britain. No one is really sure whether Geoffrey based his book mostly on old legends, or simply made it up. Some historians even doubt whether Arthur existed at all.

The story began in AD 480 at Tintagel Castle in Cornwall. Arthur's mother was the wife of the Duke of Cornwall; his father was Uther Pendragon, King of the Britons.

Arthur was just 15 when he became king on his father's death. Almost at once, he started fighting the Saxons. A whole string of battles followed and Arthur won them all, with the help of his special sword, called Caliburn. (Later writers called it Excalibur, and said it was a gift from the Lady of the Lake.)

Apart from his special sword, Arthur was said to have a spear called Ron.

Arthur went on to marry Guinevere, the most beautiful woman in the whole island. But he was not satisfied with his victories against the Saxons: next, he decided to invade Europe.

Starting with Norway, he went on to take Denmark and Gaul, and later defeated the Roman army in an especially bloody battle. But, while he was away, his nephew Mordred tried to take over Arthur's throne – and his queen.

So Arthur returned to Britain and met Mordred's army at the battle of Camblam. Mordred was killed – but Arthur himself was badly wounded.

His supporters carried him off to the Isle of Avalon. Some later writers said that he died there and was buried in AD 542. Others said that he did not die at all, but was just sleeping, until his country needed him again.

King Arthur is supposed to have had links with all these places.

A French poet first mentioned Camelot in the 12th century. It was supposed to have been Arthur's castle. Ever since, people have been looking for it.

That is not quite the end of the story. In 1191, after Geoffrey wrote his book, the monks at Glastonbury were rebuilding their **monastery** after a bad fire. About two metres below ground, they found a huge stone slab, with Arthur's name carved on it.

Even further down, they came across a tree trunk containing the bones of a big man and a skull which had been wounded in ten places. They said it was King Arthur. It seemed as if he had been tracked down at last. But the story was not over yet!

People were soon accusing the monks of lying. It was all done, some people said, as a gimmick to raise money to rebuild their monastery: they thought that the whole thing was a big hoax.

Another false trail. Guinevere was said to have given Arthur a round table as a wedding present. But this one, at Winchester, was not made until the 14th century.

1 Read the story of King Arthur carefully.
a) Write down any parts which you do not believe and explain why you do not believe them.
b) What *do* you believe about the story?

2 The picture on page 5 was painted in the 14th century and Arthur wears the clothes of that time. If he existed, he would have looked more like the Saxon warrior on page 60. Make your own drawing of Arthur in one of the scenes from his story.

3 a) Draw the map on page 58.
b) If Arthur really was connected with *all* the places shown, what sort of army must he have had?
c) Find out the place nearest you which is linked with King Arthur. Write down any stories connected with it.

4 a) One writer said it was 'ridiculous' to try to work out who Arthur was. What do you think?
b) Write down all the reasons you can think of why people should still be fascinated by King Arthur. (The cartoon above gives you one clue.)

5 Nearly everything on these two pages may be untrue, yet it is included in a history book. Do you think it would have been better if we had missed it out – and why?

But we have not finished yet with King Arthur. Read on . . .!

After the legend, the truth is a little disappointing, because the truth is that there is hardly anything about Arthur that we know for certain. Our only evidence that he existed at all is printed on the right.

Was this the real 'King' Arthur – or didn't he exist at all?

Some historians do think that there really was a man called Arthur. Perhaps he was the leader mentioned by Gildas. In which case, he was very different from the person everyone thinks of as Arthur. He would have been a leader, not a king. And he would have dressed like a Saxon warrior, not like a knight.

Perhaps such a man did hold back the Saxons for a while; perhaps he led a band of horsemen into great battles in the north or west of England. We cannot be more definite than that, except to add one thing. Perhaps if people had known more about him, they would not have been so fascinated by him for over 800 years!

Journey's end? Glastonbury Abbey and Arthur's tomb – or was it all a hoax?

A   A Welsh monk called Gildas was writing in the 540s. It is the only contemporary account of what happened after the Romans left. He did not name Arthur, but he wrote this:

The Britons took up weapons so that they should not all be killed and, led by Ambrosius Aurelianus, decided to fight their enemies. Ambrosius was a modest man who, alone of the Romans, had survived the shock of such a storm. His noble parents had been killed. With the Lord's help, his men gained victory.

From that time, the Britons and sometimes the enemy won. This went on up to the year of the siege of Mount Badon. This was the last great killing of the Saxon rabble.

B   The first mention of Arthur comes in a book written by another Welsh monk called Nennius in about AD 830. We only have *copies* of this, written in the *10th century*. This part has been shortened:

Then Arthur fought against the Anglo-Saxons with the kings of the Britons, although he was the leader in battles. The first battle was at the mouth of the river Glein. . . . The eighth battle was in Fort Guinnion in which Arthur carried a picture of the Virgin Mary on his shoulders. That day, the **pagans** fled and there was a great slaughter of them. . . . The twelfth battle was on Badon Hill, in which 960 men fell in one day from one attack in which Arthur alone killed them. In all these battles, he was the winner.

C   The final mention comes in a collection of *Annals* (yearly records). These are not contemporary either. The earlier parts were first written in the 8th century, at the earliest. They include these details:

(511–537) The fight at Camlann in which Arthur and Medraut were killed.
(490–516) Battle of Badon in which Arthur carried the cross of our Lord Jesus Christ on his shoulders for three days and nights and the Britons won.

Revision

There were no newspapers in these times. If there had been, here are four headlines you might have read:

(1) SUETONIUS WINS GREAT BATTLE: REBEL QUEEN DIES
(2) GREAT NEWS FOR BATHERS – HOT SPRINGS DISCOVERED IN BRITAIN!
(3) ROME ATTACKED BY BARBARIANS AND PEOPLE FLEE TO THE HILLS
(4) AMAZING DISCOVERY: MONKS FIND BODY OF FAMOUS LEADER

a) Explain briefly what each of these headlines is about. Write down the date of the event, if possible.
b) Choose any one of the four events and write your own news story about it. You could make a group newspaper by adding other news stories and making up suitable advertisements and pictures.

3 This poster has been drawn to remind you of an event in Roman times.
a) What was the event and where was it held?
b) What other events took place there?
c) What was the proper name for this gladiator?
d) Draw your own poster to advertise one of these events:
i) The opening day at a new public bath.
ii) A school looking for more pupils.
iii) A fresh lot of slaves for sale in the forum.
iv) A brand new villa for sale.

2 Who said what?
Draw the grid below in your exercise book, using a pencil and ruler. Next, look at what the people underneath are saying. Your job is to work out who said what. For example, if you think a Christian would have said, 'Most of my cures are made from herbs', put a tick beside the Christian in column 1. But be careful! There is only one right answer for each bubble – and not all the people in the list are saying something!

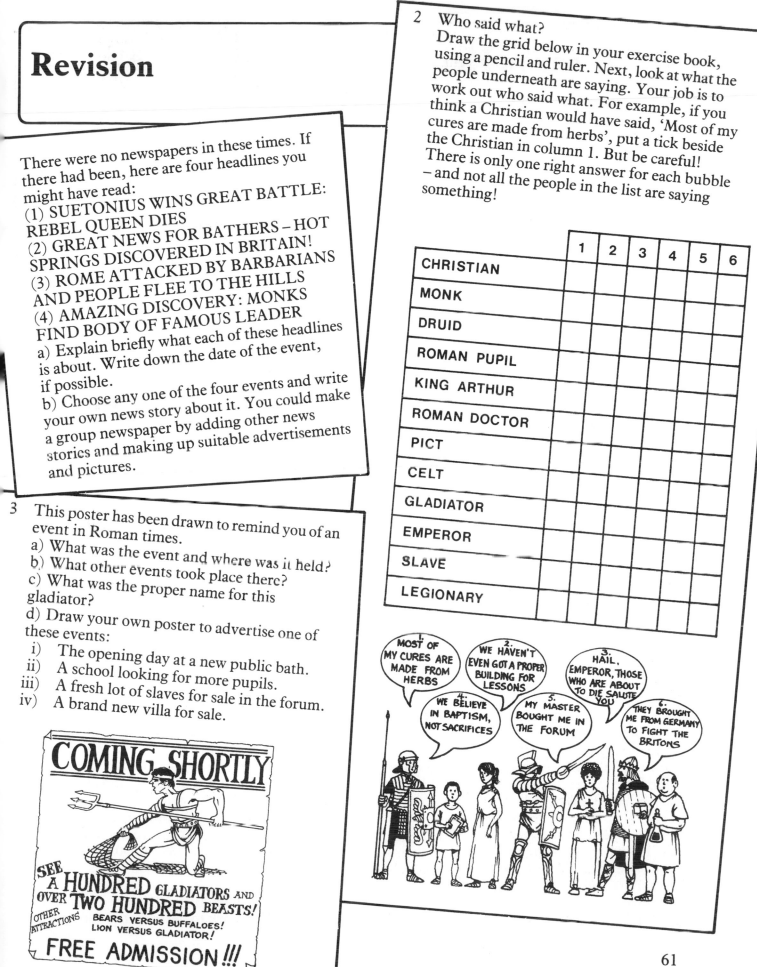

COMING SHORTLY
SEE A HUNDRED GLADIATORS AND OVER TWO HUNDRED BEASTS!
OTHER ATTRACTIONS BEARS VERSUS BUFFALOES! LION VERSUS GLADIATOR!
FREE ADMISSION !!!

	1	2	3	4	5	6
CHRISTIAN						
MONK						
DRUID						
ROMAN PUPIL						
KING ARTHUR						
ROMAN DOCTOR						
PICT						
CELT						
GLADIATOR						
EMPEROR						
SLAVE						
LEGIONARY						

1. MOST OF MY CURES ARE MADE FROM HERBS
2. WE HAVEN'T EVEN GOT A PROPER BUILDING FOR LESSONS
3. HAIL, EMPEROR, THOSE WHO ARE ABOUT TO DIE SALUTE YOU
4. WE BELIEVE IN BAPTISM, NOT SACRIFICES
5. MY MASTER BOUGHT ME IN THE FORUM
6. THEY BROUGHT ME FROM GERMANY TO FIGHT THE BRITONS

27 A Saxon Hero — Beowulf

tapestry boar
minstrel
mead meadhall

The largest building in a Saxon village was the hall. This picture shows feast night in the hall – but do not think it all looked like this! The artist has made a number of deliberate mistakes. (See question 1.)

The Anglo-Saxon village hall was like a great barn. The villagers often ate their meals together in this hall. This was where they gathered to celebrate important events, such as winning a battle.

On such a night, the hall would look a splendid sight. Smoke from the fires would drift upwards and out through the roof, while the air would be filled with the smell of wood smoke and the din of warriors enjoying their feast.

Tapestries hung from the walls where each warrior would have placed his shield, spear and helmet. Even at a feast, they had to be ready for battle. If their lord needed them, they armed themselves at once.

The lord himself sat on a raised platform at one end of the hall. Before him and the warriors were trestle tables, laden with food. Plates of **boar** meat and fish, honey cakes and bread weighed down the boards. No one went hungry on feast nights.

Few people went to sleep sober, either. A wine made from honey, called mead, was the main drink. They drank it out of glasses shaped like animal horns which could not stand up by themselves. This meant the wine had to be drunk all at once. So much was drunk that the building was often called a meadhall.

During the feasting, a **minstrel** sang songs of great deeds and famous battles long ago. Everyone knew the songs; that was part of the fun. Everyone expected stories to be told, too. Time after time, the same stories were repeated. One of them was the tale of Beowulf.

Beowulf is one of the longest poems ever written and was probably first written down around the 8th century. It is set in Denmark, but it is about the Anglo-Saxon people who came to settle in England after the Romans left.

The Anglo-Saxons probably heard it dozens of times. The poem begins with a Danish king building a famous feast hall, called Heorot. It was like the one described above but far more magnificent. Its roof was golden and even the benches were studded with gold.

Here, the warriors held their feasts. One night, a monster called Grendel came to the hall when the men were asleep. He picked up 30 of the warriors and carried them back to his lair. This happened over and over again.

A great lord called Beowulf heard about this and set out for Denmark to destroy the monster . . .

How Beowulf saved the Danes

Beowulf arrived at Heorot and offered to fight the monster. While the other fighters slept he waited at night for Grendel.....

Grendel arrived and burst into the hall. He grabbed one man and gobbled him up.

But the second one he attacked was Beowulf. The fight began.

...but he could not match Beowulf who tore an arm from the beast's body.

Their struggles shook the hall and benches were overturned. Swords could not hurt Grendel. He had put a spell on them....

The monster fled to its den to die and Beowulf hung up its arm for all to see.

Then, Grendel's mother came to Heorot to avenge her son's death. Quickly, she snatched one of the men and escaped across the haunted countryside.

Beowulf followed her to a bloodstained pool. The man's head lay nearby.

He dived in and was caught by Grendel's mother. She carried him to her cave...

...where she attacked him with a knife. But Beowulf found a giant sword and cut off her head.

Once again, Beowulf was the Danes' hero.

1   Look carefully at the picture at the top of page 62. In complete sentences, write down what is wrong in the drawing. You should find at least ten mistakes.

2   Imagine you are one of the warriors in the hall. Describe the feast you have. Remember to describe the taste of the food and the smell of the place.

3   If you were planning to attack this hall, how would you organise the attack? Use these details to help you in your planning:
* the hall is full of warriors and guarded
* there are 150 of them and 80 men with you
* you have the same weapons that they have
* the village is surrounded by a fence and a ditch; the fence is guarded.
You may draw a plan to show your ideas, if you wish.

4   a) Many years after he defeated Grendel, Beowulf had to fight a dragon which had been burning fields and houses. *Either* draw a scene from this fight *or* describe it.
b) Look in your school library for a copy of *Beowulf* and find out what happened in the fight.

28 Saxons and the Christian Religion

mission   convert
cell   Yule   Pope

The Anglo-Saxons were pagans and brought with them their own religion. They probably had many different gods although we know the names of only a few of them, such as Woden, their chief god.

We do know something about their other beliefs. They believed in giants, dragons and other strange creatures. Saxons believed that these creatures lived in wild and lonely places. If you did not please them, they would do horrible things to you.

Even some early Christians agreed that these creatures existed. One saint who went to live in the fens came across some particularly horrible dragons. They had great heads on long necks, with thin, yellow faces and filthy beards. Through their thick lips, he saw horses' teeth and their throats spat fire. The rest of the body was not too pleasant, either. They had scabby thighs, knotty knees, crooked legs and splay feet.

Journeys of the early Christian missionaries. (See question 2.)

The Saxons and Christmas

In December, the Saxons celebrated the shortest day of the year, about December 21st. Men lit bonfires to give the sun strength to bring it back to life quickly. Throughout Europe, the pagans gathered in their halls for the festival of Yule.

The Christians, of course, did not believe in worshipping the sun; they worshipped Jesus Christ. But they had a problem. Although the Bible says where Jesus was born, it does not say when. So no one was sure.

In AD 440, the Christian Church decided to fix a date for his birth. They chose a day on which the pagan peoples were already celebrating Yule. That date has become December 25th.

The pagans sacrificed oxen at Yule. The Christian Church later decided that people who became Christians could go on killing and eating oxen – to the glory of God, instead of to the devil.

A The lonely monastery at Skellig Michael, off the south coast of Ireland . . .

B . . . and Lindisfarne, which is cut off from the mainland at high tide.

The pagan Saxons crushed the Christians in most of England, although a few probably stayed true to their religion. Most fled west into areas, such as Wales, where they would be safe.

In AD 432, St Patrick set out for Ireland. He had once been kidnapped by Irish raiders. Now, he was going there on a **mission** to teach about Christ. People who wanted to give their lives to God built monasteries in wild and lonely places. Some of them overlooked the Atlantic Ocean.

And, in turn, in AD 563, a group of monks set off from Ireland on a northward journey. Their leader was an Irish prince called Columba. The place he chose to build his monastery was an equally deserted spot – the island of Iona, off the west coast of Scotland.

There, the monks lived in tiny stone rooms, called cells, meeting each other only to eat or pray. It was a hard, simple life but their example impressed people they met on their travels. They travelled down the west of Scotland and into northern Britain to spread the Christian religion.

Soon, it was not only the Britons who were being **converted**. A Saxon king called Oswald asked some of the monks from Iona to come to his kingdom to teach about Christ. In AD 634, St Aidan and a few monks came to build a monastery. The site they picked was the little island of Lindisfarne.

1 Match up the names in the left-hand column with the correct descriptions on the right.

St Patrick	Saxon king in the north
St Columba	He went to Ireland in AD 432
Aidan	He built Lindisfarne monastery
Oswald	He went to Iona in AD 563

2 Draw the map on page 64.
a) Beside the arrows, write the names of the people who made those journeys and the dates on which they made them.
b) Name the two islands where monasteries were built.

3 Look at the column about Christmas.
a) Why do you think the Church chose December 25th as Christ's birthday?
b) Do you think the Church was right to tell Christians to go on killing oxen? Give reasons for your view.

4 a) Look at evidence A and B. Which of the following words would you use to describe these places: lonely; bare; comfortable; homely; isolated; heavily populated; luxurious?
For each word you choose, explain why you picked it.
b) Why do you think the monks chose to live in such places?

Missionaries from Rome

From about AD 455 onwards, the Christians in Britain lost touch with the Christian Church in Rome. The Britons were also known as Celts so the British Christian Church was called the Celtic Church. But the Roman Church had not forgotten the Britons.

The leader of the Roman Church was called the Pope, which means 'father'. In AD 596, the Pope was a man called Gregory. He had long wanted to come to Britain himself to **convert** the pagans. Being pope, he could not come, so he chose one of his best monks to come instead. His name was Augustine.

The Roman and Celtic priests disagreed about the date of Easter – and how to cut their hair!

Saint Augustine arrives in Britain.

It was a major mission. The journey took a year and 40 monks went with Augustine. Nothing like it was ever seen again in Saxon Britain. At first, all went well.

In AD 597, they landed in Kent where the local queen was already a Christian. Her husband, King Ethelbert, gave them a friendly welcome on the Isle of Thanet. However, he thought they were magicians, so he took no chances with them. He insisted on meeting them in the open air, where he felt safer.

After Augustine had spoken to the King about the Christian religion, the King gave him and his monks a house in Canterbury. He also allowed them to try to convert his people to Christianity.

But he admitted that he found their ideas too new and strange to accept all at once.

However, eventually, Ethelbert was impressed by the monks' behaviour and became a Christian himself. Later missionaries did not find their job as easy as Augustine did. But, one by one, other Saxon kings became Christians too.

The last great pagan king was King Penda of Mercia. In AD 655 he was killed in battle fighting the Christian king, Oswy of Northumbria. King Oswy also helped Christianity in another way.

Because the Celtic Church had grown separately from the Roman Church, it meant that there were two Christian churches in Britain. But they did not always agree. King Oswy knew this only too well: his wife was a Roman Christian, while he was a Celtic Christian. So he got the two sides to have a meeting in AD 664.

At this meeting, he was told that God had given the keys to heaven to St Peter. It quickly made up his mind. He was not going to risk being turned away from heaven so he became a Roman Christian. Others soon followed his example and the Christians in Britain were united once again.

They now set about converting the rest of the people to their religion. New churches and monasteries were built; where there was no church, crosses were put up instead.

A Heaven and Hell: a drawing from about 1020.

B Bede sharpening his quill pen.

1 Write each of these dates on a separate line in your book. Then, beside each, write down what happened in that year. (You may need to read pages 64–65 for some of them.) AD 432; 563; 597; 634; 655; 664

2 Answer these questions in complete sentences:
a) Why did Gregory send Augustine to Britain?
b) Why do you think the Christians wanted to convert the pagans?
c) Why were there two Christian Churches?
d) What had they disagreed about?

3 a) Draw the picture of Bede in your book.
b) Explain in your own words why Bede was so important. (There is more about him on page 94.)

4 Study evidence A carefully. Write the numbers 1, 2, 3 and 4 on separate lines in your book. Decide what is happening in each part of the picture, using the list below. Then, write the correct description beside each number. This is the list:
An angel locks the door of Hell.
St Peter welcomes souls into Heaven.
The devil punishes the wicked.
St Peter and the devil fight over one soul.

One person who went to live in one of the monasteries was a seven-year-old boy. In AD 682, he moved to a new monastery at Jarrow, where he spent the rest of his life.

As a monk, he had to attend all the services held in the church and obey all the monks' rules. But all monks had to do this: this man also spent much of his time doing something else.

This man's name was Bede and one of his great loves was writing. From the age of 30 until he died when he was 58, he spent his time writing books on religion. He finished the last one just minutes before he died.

He wrote dozens of books, but he is famous today for just one. He wrote the first history of the Church and people of Saxon England. Without it, many parts of *this* book could not have been written.

29 Buried Treasure at Sutton Hoo

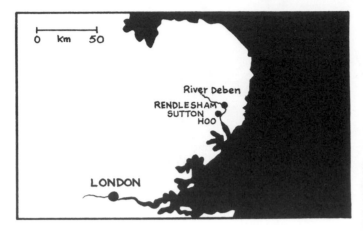

Where the treasure was found.

Archaeologists are always hoping to find more objects from Anglo-Saxon times so that we can learn more about their lives. Just once in a while, they do come across something special. The greatest find of all happened in 1939 near the Suffolk coast, at a place called Sutton Hoo.

There is a group of mounds at Sutton Hoo and, when the archaeologists opened up the largest one, they discovered the outline of a ship. The wood had rotted away long before but it had turned the sandy soil a darker colour. All that was left were the rusty remains of the nails which had held it together.

The ship itself had measured 27.5 metres long and 4.5 metres wide. It did not have a mast or sail; instead, 38 oarsmen would have rowed it. It had been buried just over ½ kilometre from the nearest river.

That was not all. In the centre of the ship a wooden burial chamber had been placed. The earth on top had made it collapse but the contents were still there, covered with soil. And these contents were amazing. What the archaeologists had dug up was the richest hoard of treasure ever found in Britain.

There was jewellery, such as a gold belt buckle, and 37 French gold coins, along with some gold **'blanks'**. There were silver bowls and silver parts of drinking horns; there was a huge silver dish with some chain mail buried under it. And much, much more besides.

A Above: the outline of the ship.

B Below: the parts of a sword which were found.

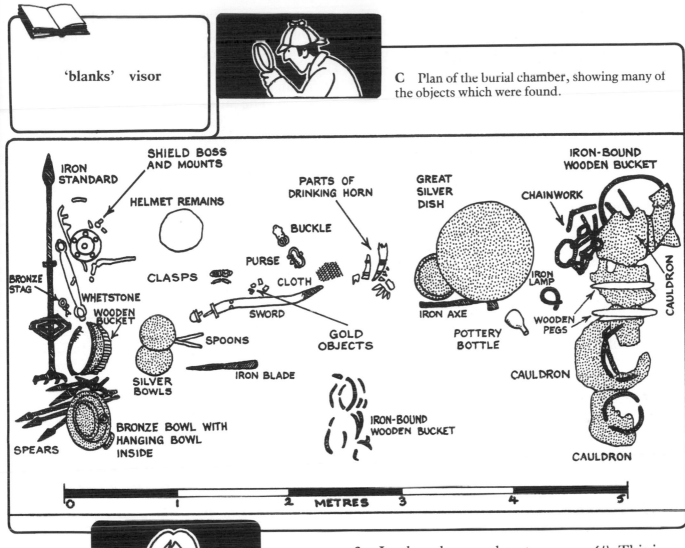

'blanks'   visor

C   Plan of the burial chamber, showing many of the objects which were found.

1   Copy out and fill in the gaps:
Archaeologists digging at _____ _____ in Suffolk in the year _____ found the remains of a _____. In the centre of it, there was a burial _____ which contained a valuable hoard of treasure. It included gold jewellery and _____, as well as silver _____ and chain _____.

2   a) Draw the plan of the burial shown above.
b) List all those objects found which were *not* mentioned on page 68.
c) What sort of person might have owned:
(i) an iron standard; (ii) a helmet and shield;
(iii) so many valuable objects?
d) If there were a body, where would you expect it to have been? Put an X on your plan on your chosen spot.

3   Look at the sword parts on page 68. This is what it would have looked like:

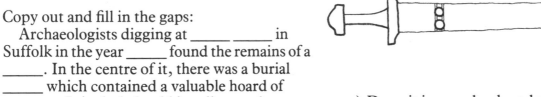

a) Draw it in your book and write in the numbers of the pieces where you think they should be.
b) Look in a library book to see if you got it right! Then, write down any mistakes you made.

4   Discuss these questions before you write down your answer. What can you work out from these facts: (a) the ship was over ½ kilometre from water; (b) there were gold 'blanks' in the mound; (c) there was a burial chamber?

There was great wealth in the mound at Sutton Hoo but one thing was missing. There was no body, not even any bones. But soil tests showed that an animal or human being *might* have been buried there. If so, the likeliest place was beside the sword.

Many people think that all the goods must have belonged to a great king. After all, only a king would have been likely to own some of the objects. The question everybody likes to ask is: Whose wealth was it?

The trouble is that people come up with different answers. The gold coins provide the best clue to a date. The latest of these coins date from the 620s. Several other objects, such as a great silver dish, were made earlier.

Many of these objects came from Scandinavia, where there were also ship burials. But the coins, for instance, came from Gaul. Perhaps they were the result of selling British slaves abroad.

The helmet is one of the objects with a Swedish design. It is made of iron, covered with bronze. The **visor** was inlaid with silver wires and precious red stones were set in it. The head was covered with beautiful designs, with more silver wires.

Many people think that the mound was in memory of one of the greatest East Anglian kings, called Redwald. He died in about 625 and had been High King of the Saxons. He had become a Christian but still went on worshipping pagan gods, too. The Sutton Hoo treasure would fit such a man: only pagans buried their dead with their possessions, yet some of the objects were Christian.

There is an even more obvious link between Sutton Hoo and *Beowulf*. Some of the things described in the poem are very similar to those found at Sutton Hoo.

That is not all. Just over 6 kilometres away from Sutton Hoo is the village of Rendlesham, where the East Anglian kings had their palace. These East Anglian kings were originally Swedish.

Even that may not be the end of the story. Two of the other mounds at Sutton Hoo were found to contain the remains of bodies. A third one had another ship buried in it. There may be even more to look forward to – some mounds have not yet been opened.

B A scene from one of the panels on the helmet. It was padded with wool and leather, rather like a crash helmet.

A Only bits of the helmet were found but experts think it looked like this. Look carefully to see the original parts.

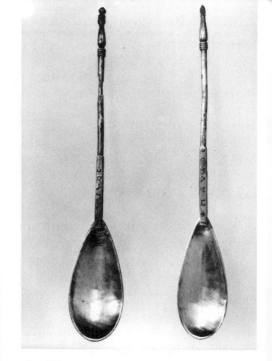

C These two spoons were also found. On one, the writing says, 'Saul'; on the other, it says, 'Paul'. Do the names remind you of a Bible story?

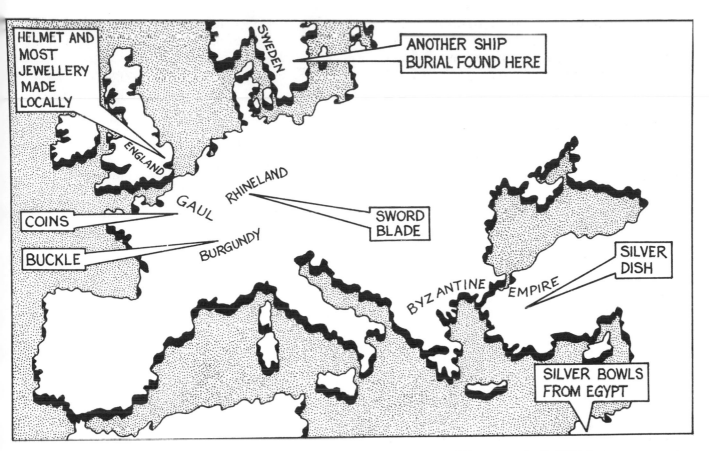

HELMET AND MOST JEWELLERY MADE LOCALLY

ANOTHER SHIP BURIAL FOUND HERE

SWEDEN

ENGLAND

GAUL

RHINELAND

BURGUNDY

COINS

BUCKLE

SWORD BLADE

BYZANTINE EMPIRE

SILVER DISH

SILVER BOWLS FROM EGYPT

This map shows where some of the objects may have come from.

D Two extracts from the poem *Beowulf*:

A boat with a ringed neck rode in the harbour, and there they laid out their lord and master, in the middle of the ship, by the mast. A mound of treasures from far countries was fetched aboard her. It is said that no boat was ever more bravely fitted out with the weapons of a warrior, equipment for war, swords and body armour. On his chest were put treasures and ornaments to travel with him on his far journey.

Then, as a sign of victory, the son of Healfdene gave Beowulf a standard worked in gold, a figured battle-banner and chest and head armour; and many admired the marvellous sword that was carried before the hero. Beowulf drank with the company in the hall. He had no cause to be ashamed of such fine gifts before the fighting men!
I have not heard that many men at arms have given four such gifts of treasure more openly to another at the mead. At the crown of the helmet was a rim, with wire wound round it, to stop the hardened blade from shattering it, when the warrior must go out against grim enemies.

1   Explain the meaning of each of these words: pagan; archaeologist; 'blanks'; standard; slave; visor; cauldron; hoard.
2   Only a king would have been likely to own some of the objects listed below. Decide which ones and explain why you chose them: helmet; sceptre; bucket; coins; iron standard; silver dishes; sword.
3   Explain in your own words why many people think the mound may be a memorial to King Redwald.
4   a) Draw the map above.
    b) How do you think these objects came to England? Think of *at least* two ways.
5   Read evidence D. List the ways in which this description fits what was found at Sutton Hoo.
6   Look at the scene from the helmet (evidence B). Draw this in your book and complete it as you think it might have looked.

71

Just some of the household gadgets which a Saxon housewife had to do without.

GAS COOKER

WASHING MACHINE

VACUUM CLEANER

FRIDGE

TINNED FOOD

compensation
handfasting
bridegroom   bride
wed

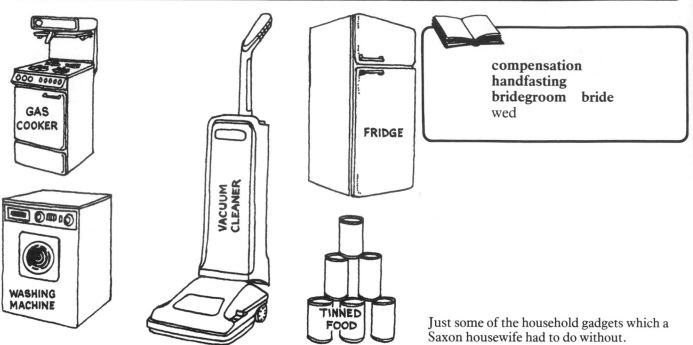

A   A Saxon woman carrying out a household chore.

Marriage amongst the ancient Britons had been a pretty simple matter. A man saw a girl he liked and just rode off with her. But it could cause problems: the family arguments could go on for years afterwards!

The Saxons took a different view of marriage. Girls played a large part in running the household. So, if a girl got married, her father expected to get some sort of **compensation** for losing her.

King Ethelbert of Kent laid down laws about it. Anyone taking a girl away by force had to pay £2.50 to her 'owner' plus a sum to be agreed later. (You could keep a married woman for nothing, as long as you found her husband someone to replace her.)

It usually worked like this. The families met to agree on the marriage and fix the price for the **bride**. The money was then handed over at the **handfasting** ceremony. The bargain was sealed with a drink and a kiss.

All this could happen years before the couple got married, but it was a very important ceremony. The money given to the girl's father was called a 'wed', which is where our word 'wedding' comes from. The girl was also given a ring which she wore on her right hand.

TO CURE A CHILD OF FEVER, PUT HIM IN AN OVEN OR ON THE ROOF.

TO CURE SOMEONE WHO IS MAD, BEAT HIM WITH A PORPOISE SKIN.

TO STOP BLEEDING, DRY HORSE DUNG. SPREAD IT ON A LINEN CLOTH AND WRAP IT ROUND THE WOUND.

At the wedding itself, the **bridegroom** moved the ring from the bride's right hand to her left hand. First, he held the ring briefly over her thumb and first two fingers, as he said, 'In the name of the father . . . in the name of the son . . . in the name of the Holy Ghost.' Finally, he said 'Amen' as he slipped the ring on the bride's third finger. This is where a Christian woman wears her wedding ring today.

One thing, however, has changed. A Saxon bride's father gave the groom one of her slippers and he immediately hit her over the head with it. This was to show everyone that he was her master.

Once she was married, a Saxon woman was never short of household jobs. A rich man's wife might have slaves to do the work, but most housewives did all the chores themselves. A Saxon wife had to:

* bake the bread
* do the rest of the cooking
* brew the family's ale
* keep the fire going
* keep the house clean
* wash the clothes
* spin thread, weave cloth and make clothes
* look after chickens and young animals
* help to thresh the corn
* deal with sickness

Of course, the men and boys would be busy themselves with farmwork while she was doing the chores, but it still seems like a hard life. After all, she had no modern gadgets to help her.

But, in some ways, she was better off than wives of later times. The law made it quite clear that no woman could be forced to marry a man whom she disliked. And, at least in early Saxon times, she could always get a divorce. Above all, she could own land and possessions and choose what to do with them.

Women had to look after anyone in the family who was ill. They had some strange cures.

Perhaps this does not sound so strange today. After all, married women now have possessions of their own. But Saxon women lost some of their freedom when the Normans came and, many centuries later, women had to fight hard to get it back. Only in our own century have women got as much freedom as they had in the days of Beowulf.

1 a) The picture at the top of page 72 shows five things which a Saxon woman did not have. Write each one down on a separate line. Then, beside each, write down what you think they used instead.
   b) Evidence A shows the answer to one of these problems. What do you think the woman is doing?
2 a) Why were fathers paid when a girl got married?
   b) Why were Saxon women better off than women in later times?
3 Look at the picture above. Which two of these 'cures' do you think were dangerous? Give reasons for your choices.
4 Do you think Ethelbert's law was a fair one? Explain how you made your mind up.
5 Answer this question in at least two paragraphs: Do you think Saxon women were better or worse off than housewives today?

31 Crime and Punishment

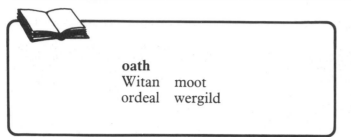

oath
Witan   moot
ordeal   wergild

In Saxon times, Britain was divided up into separate kingdoms and each had its own king. These kings made the laws, although a group of advisers helped them. These people were supposed to be clever, so they were called the Witan. It means 'wise men'.

Laws had to be clear and straightforward because there was no police force to deal with crimes. So the villagers themselves tried to make sure that people did no wrong. Villages were very small, so people all knew each other.

In early Saxon times, if someone was accused of a crime, he had to attend a village meeting, called a moot. If the accused person admitted that he had done the crime, he would be punished.

But if he said he hadn't done it, he would have to prove that he was innocent. He did this first by finding people who were willing to make an **oath** that he was innocent. Making the oath was a serious matter: you had to put your hand on a cross while you made it.

Usually, the accused person had to find 12 people who would do this. If he found them he went free. If he could not, then he might have to go through another test, called an ordeal.

This was a physical test, arranged by the Church. The idea was that God would protect an innocent person. Only the guilty would suffer.

The most common punishment for those found guilty was a fine. How much the guilty person paid depended on what he had done and who had suffered. Laws went into great detail about this. It was a bit like a price list!

The fine was called a wergild. If a person had been killed, the wergild had to be paid to their family. Some wergilds were so expensive that the criminal could not possibly pay. Instead, he became the slave of the family he had wronged.

ORDEAL BY COLD WATER

THE ACCUSED PERSON WAS TIED UP AND PUT INTO A POOL BLESSED BY A PRIEST.

IF HE SANK MORE THAN 1·7 METRES, HE WAS INNOCENT...

...BUT, IF HE FLOATED, HE WAS GUILTY. IT MEANT GOD HAD REJECTED HIM.

ORDEAL BY HOT WATER

THE PERSON PLUNGED HER HAND INTO BOILING WATER UP TO THE WRIST TO PICK UP A STONE. (FOR A SERIOUS CRIME, IT WAS UP TO THE ELBOW.)

SHE CARRIED THE STONE 2·7 METRES, THEN HER HAND WAS BANDAGED.

AFTER THREE DAYS, THE BANDAGES WERE TAKEN OFF. IF THE HAND WAS CLEAN AND HAD BEGUN HEALING, SHE WAS INNOCENT. IF NOT, SHE WAS GUILTY.

Fines were not the only punishment. Thieves might have a hand or foot cut off. Sometimes, they were put to death. Slaves were treated worst of all. One female slave was burned to death for stealing while a male slave was stoned to death.

A   The cost of crime in Saxon times.

PRICES VARIED.......FOR PEOPLE.........AND PARTS OF PEOPLE.

1500 SHILLINGS

100 SHILLINGS

20 SHILLINGS

50 SHILLINGS

10 SHILLINGS

SHILLING

B   Two punishments for a Saxon criminal.

1   Explain the meaning of each of these words: Witan; wergild; moot; ordeal.

2   Answer these questions in full sentences:
   a) Explain how trials by ordeal worked.
   b) Why did Saxons use them?
   c) Why was the Church involved in them?
   d) Why do you think people did not lie when making an oath?

3   Look at evidence B. Which *two* punishments are shown here?

4   There was one other trial by ordeal – the ordeal by hot iron. In church, the accused person had to pick up a red-hot iron and carry it 2.7 metres. It weighed ½ kilo or 1½ kilos, depending on the crime. Draw a picture strip for this ordeal, similar to the one on page 74.

5   a) Copy out evidence A.
   b) Do you think these 'prices' were fair or not?
   c) Suppose we still had the wergild system today. What price would *you* fix for (i) a hand; (ii) a leg; (iii) an eye; (iv) both hands; (v) death; (vi) a big toe? (Be reasonable!) When you have made your list, compare your prices with other people's.

32 The Vikings are Coming!

Monks hated the Vikings for destroying churches but the Vikings were pagans. So they saw nothing wrong in stealing from a church. Above: the ruins of Lindisfarne today; on the left: Viking warriors.

> AD 793. IN THIS YEAR FIERCE, TERRIBLE WARNINGS CAME OVER THE LAND OF NORTHUMBRIA AND TERRIFIED THE PEOPLE. THERE WERE VERY GREAT WHIRLWINDS, LIGHTNING STORMS, AND FIERY DRAGONS WERE SEEN FLYING IN THE SKY. THESE SIGNS WERE FOLLOWED BY GREAT FAMINE. SHORTLY AFTER, ON JUNE 8TH, THE HEATHEN MEN DESTROYED GOD'S CHURCH ON LINDISFARNE THROUGH BRUTAL ROBBERY AND SLAUGHTER. (The *Anglo-Saxon Chronicle*)

Despite all the warning signs, it is unlikely that the monks on Lindisfarne were very worried on the morning of June 8th. The attack came suddenly. The raiders would have rushed up from the sea and burst into the building. The monks' prayers were no defence against axes and swords.

The attackers had come to steal the gold and silver treasures of the church. They even dug up altars to get them. Monks who tried to stop them were just cut down; others were taken away in chains; some were drowned in the sea. Monks are not trained fighters; in any case, they had little to fight with.

It was a giant smash-and-grab raid and, when it was over, the attackers piled their loot into their black ships and probably sailed straight home.

Behind them, they left a church splattered with the monks' blood and robbed of its treasures. 'Never before,' wrote one monk, 'has such terror appeared in Britain.'

The people who brought this 'terror' were the Vikings. They lived in countries which we now call Norway, Denmark and Sweden. Their attacks came in the summer months when the North Sea was calmer; before winter came, they sailed home.

There were great riches in the British monasteries. In the next year, the Vikings were back to get more of them. This time, their target was the monastery at Jarrow, where Bede had lived.

But the monks were ready for them and had prepared themselves for a struggle. There was bitter fighting and many Vikings were killed; many of their ships were destroyed. The Viking leader was captured and killed by being pushed into a snake pit. It was to be a rare success for the British.

Within about 40 years, the Viking raids had become annual events; British leaders were killed and monasteries reduced to rubble. In 851, a huge fleet of 350 ships attacked the south of England, including London. But that year saw another change, too.

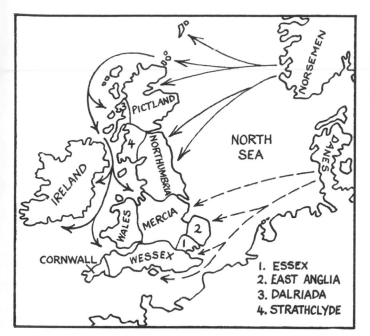

A A tombstone from Lindisfarne, carved in about AD 793.

Viking attacks.

For the first time, one group of Vikings came to Britain and stayed. They spent the winter on the Isle of Thanet in Kent. In 866, even larger numbers came. They now had a new aim. They wanted land, not loot. They had come to conquer Britain.

They probably stayed because they were short of farming land at home. Their own countries had large areas of mountains, forests and heath which were not suitable for farming. The rich soil of East Anglia must have been tempting.

One by one, the Saxon kingdoms were overrun by Vikings; by the 870s, only one kingdom was still holding out against them. It was the kingdom of Wessex.

They may have looked frightening and had strange names, but the Vikings were really hard workers – and bathed more often than the Saxons did!

1 Match up the dates on the left with the correct event from the right.

793	Vikings spent the winter in Thanet
794	Vikings attacked Lindisfarne
851	Huge numbers of Vikings came
866	Vikings attacked Jarrow

2 a) Draw the map above.
b) Shade in those areas which the Vikings had overrun by the 870s.

3 Look at the grey strip on page 76, and read about the *Anglo-Saxon Chronicle* on page 94.
a) Why did the writer believe there were 'signs' in the sky?
b) Is the writer biased for or against the Vikings? How can you tell?
c) Why was the writer biased?

4 Look at evidence A above.
a) What two weapons are the Vikings carrying?
b) Why is the date important?

5 All the written accounts of the raids were written by monks.
a) Why do you think only monks wrote about it?
b) Why does this make it hard for us to be sure about what happened?

6 Imagine you are a monk at Lindisfarne. After the attack, you wish to warn the monks at Jarrow so they are prepared. Write in detail about what happened to you and give advice on how the Jarrow monks can get ready.

In the whole of English history, only one king has been called 'Great'. It was Alfred, King of Wessex from 871 to 899. He was not called 'Great' until the 17th century but modern writers still agree that he *was* great. As you read the next four pages, try to decide what you think were his greatest achievements.

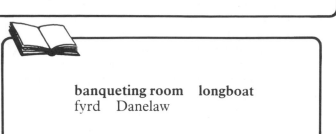

banqueting room   longboat
fyrd   Danelaw

1 Alfred asked Bishop Asser to come to Wessex. He later wrote a *Life of Alfred* and these extracts are from it:

Chapter 1
In the year of Our Lord 849, Alfred, king of the Anglo-Saxons, was born in the royal household called Wantage, in the shire called Berkshire.

Chapter 2
His mother was called Osburh, a very religious woman, noble by birth and character . . .

Chapter 22
He was loved by his father and mother, and by everyone else, with a great love. As he grew up he became more beautiful than all his brothers, and more pleasing in his looks, his words and his ways. From his cradle, his mind was filled with a longing for wisdom; unfortunately, because of the carelessness of his parents and tutors, he did not learn to read until he was at least twelve years old. But he listened closely to Saxon poems, day and night, and learned them by heart.

Chapter 23
One day his mother held out a book of Saxon poetry to show to him and his brothers. She said, 'I will give this book to whoever learns it first.' Alfred was inspired by these words – or, rather, by God – and attracted by the beautiful initial letter of the book. He replied to his mother before his brothers had a chance to speak:

'Will you really give this book to one of us – to the one who can understand it and repeat it back to you first?'

Smiling, she said she would. Taking the book out of her hand, he took it at once to his master, who read it. When it was read, he went back to his mother and repeated it.

Much of Alfred's life was spent in defending Wessex against the Vikings. In the 12th century, writers first mentioned two things which happened to Alfred during the fighting. (See page 79.)

2 Alfred is the only English king to be called 'the Great'.

3 This statue of Alfred is at Winchester. It was put up in 1901.

4 This story is from the Annals (yearly records) of St Neots and was written in the 12th century:

One day a peasant woman was making loaves and the King was sitting by the fire tending his bow and arrows and other weapons. But when the poor woman saw that the loaves she had put over the fire were burning, she ran up and took them off.

And she scolded the King, saying, 'Look there, man! You can see the loaves are burning and you've not turned them, though I'm sure you'd be the first to eat them nicely done!' The miserable woman little thought that this was King Alfred who had fought so many wars against the pagans and won so many victories.

5 William of Malmesbury wrote this, also in the 12th century:

Not long after, coming out of hiding, he tried an experiment. Accompanied only by one of his most faithful followers, he entered the tent of the Danish King, disguised as a minstrel. Once inside the **banqueting room**, there was no secret that he did not pay close attention to, both with his eyes and ears.

6 Alfred letting the cakes burn. This picture was made in the 19th century.

7 A beautiful Saxon jewel, just over 6 centimetres long. Round the edge is this writing: 'Alfred ordered me to be made'.

1 Some of the pictures and extracts on these two pages *may* be evidence about King Alfred. Take each extract and drawing and answer these questions about it:
a) When was it written or made?
b) Is it evidence or not? Give reasons for your answer.
c) Why was it written or made?
d) If it *is* evidence, is it *reliable* evidence? (Read page 4 again before answering this.)
e) What can we learn – if anything – about King Alfred from the writing or drawing?

For example, cartoon 2 is not evidence. It was drawn in 1984 and the artist had never met Alfred. It was drawn simply to amuse anyone reading this book.

2 Which of the following words would you expect to describe a king called 'the Great': kind; generous; strong; brave; tall; a great warrior; intelligent; religious; just; good looking; without mercy?

For each word you choose, explain why you picked it.

3 Write about your early life, in the way that Asser wrote about Alfred. Include at least one story about yourself which you think teaches a reader something important about you.

England was shared between Alfred and the Vikings. The Vikings were mainly from Denmark so their area was called the 'Danelaw' because people living there had to obey the Danes' law.

By the time Alfred was growing up, the Vikings were starting to settle in England. In 870, they began to attack Wessex. Although they were stopped at a battle at Ashdown in January 871, it was only a temporary setback.

In the months that followed, Alfred's brother, Aethelred, died and Alfred became King of Wessex. After Ashdown, there followed a whole string of battles and the Vikings won them all.

They must have thought they were unstoppable. All that stood between them and complete victory was Wessex. And Wessex was led by Alfred, who was only about 22 years old.

Alfred tried everything. He even paid them money to go away, though he knew it was not a lasting solution. He was right. In the early days of 878, they were back.

No one expected the Vikings to attack in the middle of winter. They always came in summer-time. This time it was different. They launched a surprise attack on the Saxons at Chippenham. Many Saxons were killed; the rest fled.

Alfred's hiding-place was on the Isle of Athelney in Somerset. In those days, it was completely cut off by marshes. There, he built a fort. However, although he was safe, he could not protect the rest of his kingdom. But he gradually built up his army again with men from the areas around.

By May 878, he was ready and his new army marched out towards Salisbury Plain to meet the Vikings. They, led by their king, Guthrum, set out from Chippenham to meet him.

The result was the battle of Edington – and Alfred won. The Vikings were so well beaten that they had to accept Alfred's peace terms. They were not harsh because Alfred knew it was not the end of the Viking threat.

So an agreement was reached: the Vikings kept north-eastern England, while Alfred ruled Wessex in the south.

Some of the ways in which Viking villages got their names. Spellings have sometimes changed over the years.

HE ENCOURAGED EDUCATION.....

...AND EVEN TRANSLATED A BOOK FROM LATIN INTO ANGLO-SAXON HIMSELF.

HE TOOK THE BEST LAWS FROM OTHER KINGDOMS AND MADE NEW LAWS FOR HIS OWN.

Some of Alfred's many other achievements.

But the Vikings were still a danger. If Alfred was to hold on to Wessex, he had to be able to defend it. This is what he did:

1   Alfred built new ships

If the Vikings did raid again, Alfred had to stop them landing. So he ordered new ships to be built. They were **longboats**, like the Viking ships, but twice the size, with 60 or more oars each.

2   Alfred built forts along the coast

Just in case they did land, he started building a string of forts across southern England. If there was an attack, villagers could move there for safety. By the time Alfred died, no villager was more than a day's march (about 32 kilometres) from a safe place.

3   Alfred improved the army

Most important of all, Alfred improved his part-time army. It was called the fyrd. Most of his men were not trained fighters at all: they were farm labourers. They did not like fighting far from home in summer. It meant they might not get home for harvest-time.

So Alfred split his forces in two. Half the fyrd was on active service, manning the forts and ready for action. Meanwhile, the other half stayed at home and got on with the farming. Every so often, they swapped over.

The policies worked. Alfred took over London in 886 and, when the Vikings attacked again in 892, his fyrd was able to beat them off. Before he died in 899, Alfred was calling himself 'King of the Anglo-Saxons'.

It was a title which he had well earned.

1   Write out these dates in order. Put each on a separate line:
899; 878; 871; 892; 886.
Beside each date, write down what happened in that year.

2   If you were Alfred and wanted to re-arm the fyrd, which of these weapons would you give them: (a) an axe; (b) a sword; (c) machine-gun; (d) pitchfork; (e) shield; (f) stones?
(Look at the Vikings' weapons on page 76 first.) For each weapon, explain why you would or would not use it.

3   a) Draw the map on page 80.
b) Each fort is now a large town. Using a modern atlas, name each of the forts.
c) Look at the drawing on page 80. Using the atlas, write down at least two place-names ending in each of the ways shown.

4   When Alfred died, this is what the *Anglo-Saxon Chronicle* said about him:

Alfred, son of Aethelwulf, passed away, six nights before All Saints' Day. He was king over all the English, except for that part which was under Danish rule; and he held that kingdom for one and a half years less than thirty.

It was a very brief account for a great king! See if you can do better. Write your own entry for the Chronicle when Alfred died and mention some of his achievements.

81

34 Reading and Writing

freemen
quill   parchment
illuminated manuscript
Runic alphabet

Alfred did not just want to beat the Vikings. He had other aims, too. One of his dearest wishes was to educate his people. In particular, he wanted the priests and important people to be much better educated.

He encouraged teachers to come from Europe to help him. It was the biggest scheme of its time. All important books, including the Bible, were translated into Anglo-Saxon. Then, all the sons of **freemen** were taught to read the language.

Alfred himself translated a number of books into Latin and, during his reign, monks began writing the Anglo-Saxon Chronicle. It was a history of what happened in England from Christ's birth onwards. No other country had anything like it.

The monks played an important part in all of this. They provided most of the teachers, and most of the pupils were studying to become monks themselves. In the palace schools, started by King Alfred, boys learned how to hunt and wrestle, as well as reading and writing.

Most Saxon children did not go to school. Their parents taught them all they needed to know.

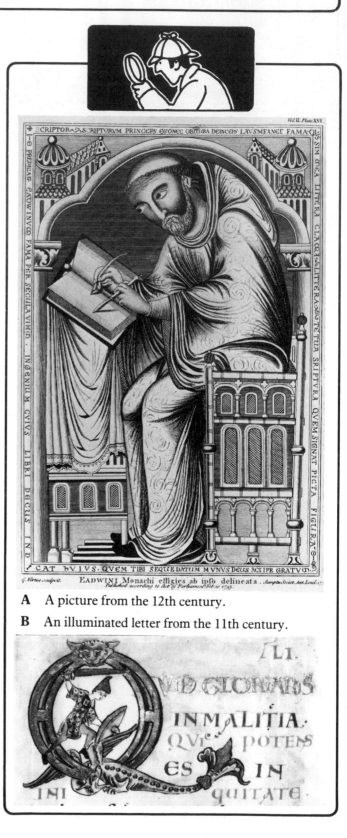

A   A picture from the 12th century.

B   An illuminated letter from the 11th century.

C The Saxons brought their own alphabet called the Runic alphabet to Britain and used it, as well as the Latin alphabet. This picture shows how a Welshman translated the Runic alphabet in the 9th century.

But the monks also had another vital task. Schools needed books. There were no printing presses in those days so monks had to write every book out by hand.

It was a slow job. There were no pens, such as we have today. Instead, the feathers of a large bird, like a goose, were sharpened to make quills. There was no paper either; they used parchment. This was animal skin which had been smoothed and stretched.

The monks took great care to make these books as beautiful as possible. These were not books which would be read and thrown away, or given to jumble sales! They were making something as perfect as possible, to last for centuries.

The results are beautiful. They took special care with the capital letters which started each page.

They painted pictures around them in expensive coloured inks. We call these books 'illuminated manuscripts'.

NO, BROTHER THOMAS, NOT THE WHOLE GOOSE!

1 Copy out and complete this paragraph:
   King _____ encouraged teachers to come to England from Europe. He also had various books translated into _____ - _____. Monks began writing 'The Anglo-Saxon _____' during his reign. They also taught in the _____ schools which Alfred began, and wrote books. Some of these were beautifully coloured and are called _____ _____.

2 Look at evidence A.
   a) What sort of person is this man and what is he doing?
   b) Look at the two objects he is holding. What do you think they are used for?

3 Look carefully at evidence B.
   a) Which letter do you think this is?
   b) Draw and colour an illuminated letter for the first letter of one of your names.

4 Look at evidence C and read the caption.
   a) Which modern letters were not represented in the Runic alphabet?
   b) Why do you think there are no curved letters?
   c) Write out a sentence, using the Runic alphabet. When you have finished, swap it with a friend and try to work out what each other has written.

35 Sports and Pastimes

ancestor
fowling   tafl
saga

Most Saxon and Viking children never went to school. They started helping their parents at a very early age. But their lives were short. On average, people only lived to about 30, so there was not much time for enjoying themselves.

Yet, there were winter evenings when there was less farmwork to do and the attacking season was over. Then, there was time for amusement. Feasts were popular and there was always a great deal of drinking going on. After the food, there was story-telling and singing and dancing.

Outdoor sports were popular. Richer Saxons enjoyed horse-riding; hunting and fowling, to catch birds, were also common. There were kinds of ball games, too. And travelling entertainers came and performed in the villages: some were jugglers; others brought tamed wild animals.

We know much less about their indoor games. One Saxon board-game was called tafl, which involved one person trying to move a piece on the board while the other person tried to attack it. The Vikings enjoyed playing draughts and chess, using pieces made of bone.

Young children played games which trained them for adult life. Archaeologists have found small swords and axes, which children must have used to play 'war games'. Young Viking boys learned to wrestle and swim to prepare them for later life.

The easiest form of entertainment was story-telling. Tales were told of ancient heroes and people loved making up poems. Many of the Viking tales were about what their **ancestors** had achieved. They were stirring stories of famous men and brave deeds, told around the fires in the long winter evenings. These long stories are called 'sagas'.

SAXON MUSICAL INSTRUMENTS

A   The Saxons loved telling riddles. Here are two of them:

A certain object grew in the corner; it rose and expanded and threw up a crust! A proud wife carried off that boneless wonder; the daughter of a King covered that swollen thing with a cloth.

My nose is pointed downwards; I crawl along and dig in the ground. I go as I am guided by the grey enemy of the forest, and by my lord, who walks stooping at my tail. He lifts me and presses me on and sows in my track. As I advance, on one side of me there is green, while on the other my black track is clear.

B   One violent Viking sport was horse-fighting. This picture is from a Swedish stone-carving.

1   The following groups of letters give you the names of Saxon and Viking amusements, but the letters have been muddled up. Work out what each one is and write a sentence about it:
(i) CGNDNAI; (ii) REHSO-GRINID;
(iii) FLAT; (iv) GLINUJGG; (v) GLOWFIN.

2   Two sports had a purpose besides just being fun. Which ones were they and what was the other reason for doing them?

3   Food was one great source of pleasure. At the top and bottom of this page are some of the foods eaten by the Saxons. Write the numbers in your book and work out as many of them as possible.

4   a) Read evidence A and try to work out what each riddle is describing.
b) Make up your own riddle for something else which existed in Saxon times. Then, try it out on the rest of your group and see if they can work out what it is.

5   On page 84 are drawings of some Saxon musical instruments. For each one, write down what modern instrument it is most like.

AUGUST 11TH 991 + STOP + VIKING ARMY MEETS SAXON ARMY AT MALDON IN ESSEX + STOP + SAXON LEADER BYRHTNOTH KILLED + STOP + VIKINGS WIN GREAT BATTLE + STOP

A   Background picture shows the water which the Vikings had to cross to get to the Saxons. It was not as wide in 991 as in this modern photograph. Drawings show (on left) a Viking warrior and (on right) a Saxon.

B   A Saxon described the battle soon afterwards:

Then Byrhtnoth began to place his men; he taught his warriors how they should stand and defend their ground; he told them to keep their shields straight and fear nothing. [Then] he got down among the people where he most likes to be and where he knew his bodyguard was most loyal.

Then the Viking messenger stood on the bank and boastfully spoke the Vikings' message to the Earl: 'Bold seamen have sent me to you, and told me to say that you must send treasure quickly in return for peace. We need not destroy each other.

Byrhtnoth lifted up his voice, grasped his shield and, shaking his spear, answered with anger: 'Messenger of the seamen, take back a message. Tell how there stands here with his troop an earl who is ready to guard this kingdom. You shall not win payment so easily; peace must be made with point and blade before we pay **tribute**.'

Because of the water, neither force could reach the other until the tide went out. When it did, the defenders chose a warrior, Wulfstan, to hold the bridge. When the Vikings realised they had to deal with such grim defenders, they became cunning and begged permission to pass over the ford and lead their men across.

The Earl, in his pride, began to give way to the hateful foe and [one of the Saxons] called to the warriors: 'Now the way is open to you; come quickly to meet us in battle. Only God knows who will win.'

The wolves of slaughter pressed forward. They did not care about the water, those Vikings; the seamen came to land with their lime wood shields.

There, ready to meet the enemy, stood Byrhtnoth and his men. He told them to form a wall with their shields, and hold their line against the enemy. The battle was now at hand. Now was the time when those who were doomed would fall. A shout went up, ravens went circling, the eagle greedy for dead meat. There was a cry upon earth.

They let the spears fly from their hands. Bows were busy. Point pierced shields. The rush of battle was fierce; warriors fell on both sides.

The Saxons stood firm. Byrhtnoth encouraged them and told each warrior to give his mind to war if he wanted to win glory against the Vikings.

Then one of the warriors let a dart fly from his hand, so that it pierced [Byrhtnoth] all too deeply. By his side stood a young warrior who boldly pulled out the bloody spear. He let the weapon speed back again; it drove in so hard that his lord's cruel killer lay dead on the ground.

D A 10th century stone-carving of a Viking.

Then, a fully armed man approached the Earl, meaning to seize his clothes and rings and his richly decorated sword. Byrhtnoth drew his blade and struck his armour. All too quickly, one of the seamen stopped his hand, crippling the Earl's arm. His golden hilted sword fell to the earth; he could not use his hard blade or wield a weapon.

The white haired warrior could now no longer stand firm on his feet. The Earl looked up to heaven and cried aloud: 'I thank you, ruler of nations, for all the joys I have had in this world. Grant that my soul may journey to you in peace. I pray to you that fiends of hell may not stop it.'

Then the heathen wretches cut him down. Then those who had no wish to be there turned away from the battle. Offa's sons led the flight; Godric leapt upon the horse that had belonged to his lord with trappings that he had no right to. Both his brothers galloped away; they had no taste for war, but fled to the stronghold and saved their lives.

C The Anglo Saxon Chronicle said this:

After, men made peace with the Vikings and in this year (991) it was first advised that tribute should be given to the Vikings, because of the horrors they worked along the coasts. The first payment was ten thousand pounds.

The battle of Maldon. Byrhtnoth probably had to let the Vikings cross the water if he wanted to fight them. Otherwise, they could just have sailed off with their loot.

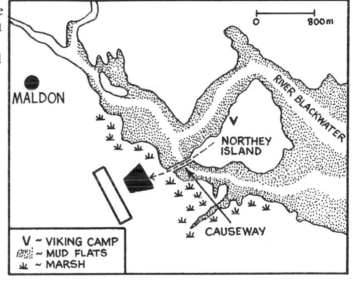

MALDON

RIVER BLACKWATER

NORTHEY ISLAND

CAUSEWAY

V ~ VIKING CAMP
~ MUD FLATS
~ MARSH

0   800m

1   Read all evidence B carefully.
   a) Is it biased for or against the Saxons? Pick out any words which show bias.
   b) According to evidence B, which weapons did each side use, and how were they used?
   c) Do you think Byrhtnoth's tactics were right? Read the caption above the map and give reasons for your views.
   d) Did he give good advice to his men? Again, give examples which prove your point.

2   a) Draw the map on this page.
   b) Decide which army is which, then colour the Vikings in blue and Byrhtnoth's army in red. Add a key to your map.

3   Look at evidence D. Draw this in your book and name each of the weapons shown.

4   a) Why was £10 000 paid to the Vikings?
   b) Do you think this was a good idea?

5   Byrhtnoth himself was over 60 years old and a huge 2.05 metres tall. Draw him with the correct costume from page 86.

court
Danegeld

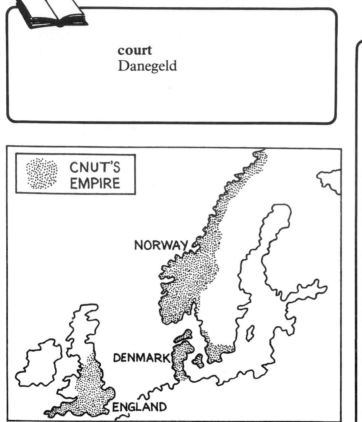

The empire of King Cnut.

In one way, the Battle of Maldon marked the beginning of the end for Saxon England. It was not the first time that money had been paid to get the Vikings to go away. But it cost the king, Ethelred, £10 000 on this occasion.

In 994, the Vikings were back. This time the price of retreat was £16 000. And so it went on for the next 20 years. People came to call the money 'Danegeld', which means 'Danish money'.

It was very expensive – and it did not work. Nearly every year, more Vikings turned up for a share of the money. Each time, the payment went up. Over 50 years, the total was something like £250 000. And that meant that the English had to pay higher taxes. No wonder they hated it.

In 1002, Ethelred thought the Vikings were plotting against him and he panicked. He ordered the death of all Vikings living in England outside the Danelaw.

A Henry of Huntingdon wrote about Cnut in the 12th century:

Cnut reigned for twenty years. Never before him was there a king in England of such greatness. At the very height of his power, he ordered his throne to be put at the seaside when the tide was rising.

He spoke to the waves, 'You are under my control as much as the land on which my throne is. There has never been anyone who has resisted my rule without being punished. I therefore command you not to rise on my land. You shall not dare to wet the clothes or limbs of your master.'

The sea rose in the usual way and wetted the feet and legs of the King without showing any respect. The King leapt up and said, 'Everyone on earth should know that the power of kings is useless and unimportant. No one deserves the name of king except God who controls heaven and earth, and sea.'

Cnut therefore never again wore the golden crown on his head but placed it above an image of the Lord which is nailed to a cross.

Cnut may not have done this because he was big-headed. He may have been proving something to his nobles. What could it have been?

One of them turned out to be the sister of Swein Forkbeard, the king of Denmark. And Swein Forkbeard decided to get his own back.

In 1013, he invaded England and destroyed Oxford and Winchester. When he died the next year, his fleet chose his son, Cnut, as king. He carried on his father's work and, by 1016, had conquered nearly all England. The English nobles had little choice: Cnut became the new king of England.

He was a strong king and brought peace to his new land. Ethelred died in 1016 and Cnut married his widow and became a Christian. Many of the churches and monasteries damaged by Viking raiders were repaired.

His empire was big for the time. It covered England and most of Scandinavia. When Cnut died, his two sons shared it out between them but both were dead within seven years.

They had no children so the English nobles met once more to pick themselves a king. Their choice was Ethelred's son, Edward. He had been quietly living in Normandy for nearly 30 years.

Edward would probably have preferred to go on with his peaceful life there. He was a very religious man who spent much of his time in prayer. People called him 'the Confessor' because he spent so much time confessing his sins to God.

Back in England, Edward continued with the sort of life he had led in Normandy. His Norman friends were rewarded with land and jobs; his **court** was like the one at which he had lived in Normandy. That was the court of Duke William, the ruler of Normandy.

None of this pleased the English nobles. They wanted a strong king who could defend their country; and they wanted a truly English king. In time, they were to find that they could not have both. And *that* opened up a whole new period in British history . . .

1 Draw this grid in your book and fill in the answers, using the clues below:

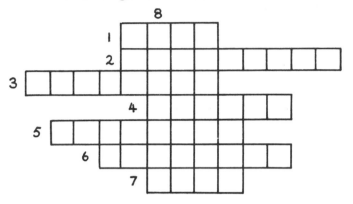

1 The son of Swein Forkbeard.
2 Edward's nickname.
3 He kept paying the Vikings to go away.
4 The battle in 991 after which payments began.
5 Duke William was ruler of this land.
6 Money paid to the Vikings.
7 What Edward spent his time confessing.
8 down tells you what to expect next!

2 a) Draw the map of Cnut's empire.
b) Read evidence A. Although this story may not be true, it shows us what people thought of the King's character. Do you think Cnut was: proud; stupid; easily persuaded; strong-minded; not proud; brave; wise; wet? Give reasons for your choices.
3 If you had been Ethelred, what long-term plans would you have made for dealing with the Vikings? Give a detailed answer.

More invaders would soon be coming.

This book covers a huge period of time, and great changes came about in the way people lived over all those years. But we should remember that Britain has changed far more *since* 1066 than it had in the thousands of years between the building of Stonehenge and the arrival of the Normans.

In 1066, there were probably only just over 1 million people living in Britain. That is less than the number of people living in just one big city nowadays. When Edward the Confessor died, there were at least three times as many sheep as there were people! Much of the land was still covered by trees and wild bears still roamed the great forests.

By 1066, more people lived in towns than in any other country in Europe. The names of those towns gave clues to the people who started them. Places such as Chester and Gloucester were started by the Romans. Their names are based on the Latin word, 'castra', which means 'a camp'. The Saxons and Vikings also gave names to villages, as we have seen.

They gave names to people, too, and many are still used today. If your name is Cook, Webster or Smith, then your ancestors probably lived in Britain in Saxon times. If your name ends in -son, there is a good chance that you are descended from Vikings!

The safety pin first appeared before the Iron Age.

Even so, three groups of invaders had left their mark on the country. The Romans, as it happened, had less effect on Britain than on most countries they conquered. Most of their buildings were destroyed or built upon in the centuries that followed.

But their roads did survive. True, they were in a bad state by 1066 but they were still the best roads that the country had – and stayed the best for centuries to come. Even today, many of the modern main roads partly follow the routes which the Romans chose.

JANUARY ~	NAMED AFTER THE ROMAN GOD JANUS. HE HAD TWO FACES, LOOKING IN OPPOSITE DIRECTIONS.
FEBRUARY ~	NAMED AFTER THE FESTIVAL OF FEBRUA.
MARCH ~	NAMED AFTER MARS, THE ROMAN GOD OF WAR.
APRIL ~	NAMED AFTER THE GODDESS APHRILIS, THE GODDESS OF LOVE.
MAY ~	NAMED AFTER THE ROMAN MOTHER-GODDESS MAIA.
JUNE ~	MAY HAVE BEEN NAMED AFTER JUNO, THE WIFE OF JUPITER, KING OF THE ROMAN GODS.
JULY ~	NAMED AFTER JULIUS CAESAR, WHO WAS BORN THEN.
AUGUST ~	NAMED AFTER THE ROMAN EMPEROR AUGUSTUS.
SEPTEMBER ~	WAS ORIGINALLY THE 7TH MONTH.
OCTOBER ~	WAS ORIGINALLY THE 8TH MONTH.
NOVEMBER ~	WAS ORIGINALLY THE 9TH MONTH.
DECEMBER ~	WAS ORIGINALLY THE 10TH MONTH.

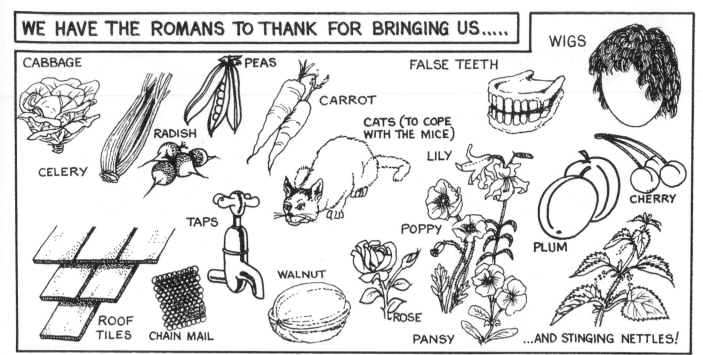

WE HAVE THE ROMANS TO THANK FOR BRINGING US.....

CABBAGE

PEAS

FALSE TEETH

WIGS

CELERY

RADISH

CARROT

CATS (TO COPE WITH THE MICE)

LILY

CHERRY

TAPS

POPPY

PLUM

ROOF TILES

CHAIN MAIL

WALNUT

ROSE

PANSY

...AND STINGING NETTLES!

The Anglo-Saxons helped shape the English language. It grew out of the language spoken by the Saxons who came and settled in England. Nearly all common English words are either Saxon or Viking.

The Saxon gods, for instance, gave us the names of four of our days of the week:

* Tiw, the god of battle, gave us Tuesday.
* Woden, the chief god, gave us Wednesday.
* Thor, the god of thunder, is Thursday.
* Frey, the goddess of crops, became Friday.

While the Saxons gave us four days, the Romans gave names for all our months. And our year begins in January because Julius Caesar decided that it should. (Until then, it had begun in March.)

In one other way, the Romans had a lasting effect on the country. They brought over a whole range of new crops and vegetables, new garden flowers and fruits. They introduced oxen to pull the ploughs. They even brought over the first cats – to cope with the mice!

The Angles gave their name to England. Julius Caesar called the islands 'Britannia' by mistake, but the name stuck – to become 'Britain'.

BRITANNIA

ANGLE-LAND

STIRRUP

BRIDESMAIDS

TUMBLER....
...BECAUSE IT TUMBLED OVER!

The Saxons gave us these.

Westminster Abbey, as it is today. On the right, the Saxon church of Bradwell-on-Sea, Essex.

The Saxons, too, made many changes. Perhaps the greatest was to make England a Christian country. Even the Christian festival of Easter is named after a Saxon goddess called Eostre. The first Archbishop was Augustine and he was based at Canterbury; the Archbishop of Canterbury is still the leading priest in the Church of England.

1   Divide your page into two columns, using a pencil and ruler. Put these headings above the columns: *Romans* and *Saxons*. In the columns, list all the objects and changes which each group of people introduced.
2   Pick out the two changes (or objects) which you think are the most important and draw them in your book. Underneath each one, explain why you think it is so important.
3   a) Copy out the diagram of the months on page 90.

They built many new churches in which to worship God. Some still remain today, although most of them have been changed a lot over the last thousand years.

The greatest of these churches was only finished just before the Normans arrived in 1066. In 1050, Edward the Confessor had begun building Westminster Abbey in London. It was to be the finest church in the land.

In January 1066, Edward died. Days later, they buried him in his new church. Before the year was out, the country would have had two new kings and the Norman age would have arrived.

b) Can you think of any better names for our months? For instance, the Saxons had their own names. May was called 'Tri-milki' because cows were milked three times a day; December was 'Winter-monat'. Can you do better? Write down ideas for at least three months.
4   Sadly, it is pretty impossible for us to taste the sort of food the Romans liked. This is because they used ingredients which we cannot make today *and* be sure we've got them right. But we can at least try! Here is a simple recipe for a seasoning called liquamen. (The Romans cooked just about everything in it!)

Take salt water and test its strength by throwing an egg into it to see if it floats; if it sinks, the water does not contain enough salt. Put fish [such as mackerel] into the salt water in a cooking pot. Add oregano and put it on a good fire until it boils. Let it cool and strain it two or three times, until it is clear.

Afterwards, you should really let it mature for two or three months at least, occasionally stirring it with a stick. And remember – this is an easy way to make it!

Revision

1 Copy this crossword into your book, then fill in the answers, using the clues below.

Clues: Across
1. Roman writer whose father-in-law was a governor of Britain. (7)
5. King Oswy became a Roman Christian because he was afraid that, if he did not, he might find the gates to heaven were _____. (4)
6. Land lying unused so that it can regain its goodness. (6)
8. These people gave their name to England.(6)
10. The Bishop who wrote a *Life of Alfred*. (5)
14. The island where Columba built a monastery. (4)
15. Some people still say that this 'king' won the Battle of Mount Badon. (6)
17. Cnut tried to hold it back! (3)
19. A metal which gave its name to an age. (4)
21. The monk who lived at Jarrow and wrote an important history book. (4)
22. One early Christian martyr was _____ Alban. (5)

Clues: Down
1. A Saxon board-game. (4)
2. The people who were living in Britain before the Romans came. (5)
3. In the 7th century, there were _____ Christian Churches in Britain. (3)
4. The pagan festival in mid-winter. (4)
7. A fight between two countries. (3)
9. The man in number 15 across was supposed to have a magic one, called Excalibur. (5)
11. A person who is owned by someone else. Rich Romans thought that you could not live without them. (5)
12. A rich Roman's country house. (5)
13. Iron Age priests who were feared and respected by the people. (6)
16. The greatest hoard of treasure ever found in Britain was discovered at Sutton _____. (3)
18. Favourite weapon of the Vikings. (3)
20. A woman who lived in a monastery, although we usually call her building a nunnery. (3)

2 It is difficult for us to be sure about much of the history of this period. As you have seen, many of the accounts were written long afterwards by people who had not been present. Often, later writers added details which may not be correct. You can see how it happens by playing this game.

Read this sentence from the *Anglo-Saxon Chronicle*:

982. Three ships of Vikings came up into Dorset, and ravaged in Portland the same year.

This is how you play:
Imagine that this was something which happened when your father was a child and he has told you about it. Now, you have decided to tell your own children about it, but it does not sound very interesting as it is. So, you decide to add one detail to it.

In the game, the first person in your group writes down the sentence, adding a suitable detail. He or she passes the paper on and each person, in turn, adds a sentence. When the paper has been all round the class, one of you can read out the final version.
What do you notice about all those extra sentences?

Writers and Sources

It is hoped that these brief background notes will be of some help to teachers. More detailed biographies may be found in such works as the *Dictionary of National Biography*.

The Anglo-Saxon Chronicle was written by English monks in various towns and tells the story of events up to the mid-12th century. There are seven different Chronicles. Only some parts were written at the time of the events they describe.

Bishop Asser (d. 909) was a monk whom King Alfred persuaded to join his court in about 885. He spent six months of each year there, helping Alfred in his studies. He was given various posts in return.

Bede (673–735) is our main source for early English history and took great care to gather material, both written and oral, for his history. His own Preface indicates many of these. However, most of his book is second-hand information and some of his sources are now lost.

Beowulf is one of our greatest early poems but has survived in only one Saxon manuscript, a copy made in about 1000. Experts still argue about when it was first composed, but the most generally quoted period is the 8th century.

Julius Caesar (c. 100–44 BC) wrote in detail about his campaigns in Gaul and the invasions of Britain. These provide the first eye-witness accounts of Iron Age Britain.

Geoffrey of Monmouth (1100–1154) is difficult to assess as a source. He claimed that his history was based on an ancient manuscript but, if this is true, it is now lost. No one really believes he made it all up, but a fanciful imagination may have made him less critical of earlier sources than other writers.

Gildas (c. 496– c. 580) was a Welsh bishop who provides the only contemporary account of life in Britain after the Romans left. However, he does complain about his own sources, saying that they were often unclear or had information missing. And he is inclined to see all the Britons' sufferings as a punishment sent by God because of their sins.

Henry of Huntingdon (1084–1155) was an archdeacon who wrote a history of England up to 1154. Many of his stories are taken from earlier manuscripts.

Marcus Quintilian (c. AD 35– c. 100) was a famous orator and teacher whose ideas had a considerable effect on the development of education throughout the Empire.

Lucius Seneca (4 BC – AD 65) wrote his *Letters from a Stoic* at the end of his life. He believed strongly in leading an upright life and bitterly condemned the pleasure-seeking of the bored Roman élite.

Cornelius Tacitus (c. AD 56– c. 115) wrote a number of histories, including a life of his father-in-law, Agricola, who was governor of Britain from AD 78 to 84. He is generally accepted as a reliable source but is biased in favour of Agricola.

William of Malmesbury (c. 1080– c. 1143) wrote about English history up to 1142. He was a monk and a librarian, who took some trouble to get his facts right. He was an eye-witness of many of the later events he described.

Glossary

abacus – a counting-frame

altar – a stand or table which plays an important part in a religious service, perhaps for sacrifices

amphitheatre – a building with seats round an open space

amputated – cut off

ancestor – a person from whom you are descended

arena – a space where contests take place

banqueting room – a room for feasts

baptism – a religious act, involving putting water on a person, to show that their sins are washed away

barbarian – a foreigner or savage

blank – a piece of metal, ready to be made into a coin

boar – wild pig

bride – a woman about to be married or just married

bridegroom – a man about to be married or just married

cavalry – soldiers who fight on horseback

cemetery – a place for burying the dead

ceremony – a special occasion

chariot – a two-wheeled cart pulled by horses

compensation – money given to make up for something else

convert – change someone from being a pagan into a Christian

court – a place where a king lives

crucified – killed by being nailed to a cross

drug – a medicine

emperor – the ruler of an empire

estate – a large piece of land

fallow – land on which no crops are growing

fertilizer – something put on soil to make plants grow better

flint – a very hard stone

freemen – men who were free of all (or most) duties to a lord

frontier – a border between two countries

government – the people who rule a country

governor – a ruler

handfasting – engagement

idol – a statue worshipped by non-Christians

javelin – a spear used as a weapon

legend – an ancient story which many people believed

legion – a part of the Roman army

lintel – a stone lying on top of two upright stones

longboat – a long ship, as those used by Vikings

mammoth – a very large kind of elephant which no longer exists

martyr – a person who dies because of what he believes in

massager – a person who rubs muscles and joints to make them work better

minstrel – a singer or musician

mission – a journey to spread the Christian faith

monastery – a building where monks or nuns live

monument – a building which reminds people of earlier people or an event

myth – a made-up story

oath – a very serious promise

pagan – a person who is not a Christian

reservoir – a place where water is collected

sacred – holy

sacrifice – something offered to a god or the act of doing it

sarcen – a large block of sandstone

sewer – a drain to carry away waste water and refuse

shield boss – a raised decoration on a shield

sickle – a tool with a short curved blade

stadium – an open space, surrounded by seats, used for sporting events

standard-bearer – a man who carried the legion's banner

stirrup – a support for a horse-rider's foot

surveyor – a person who measures and plans roads

tapestry – a cloth with a picture woven on it

tax – money paid by people to their rulers

temple – a holy building

torque – a twisted band to go round the neck

tribute – money paid by one people to another in order to get peace

turf – grass, complete with its roots

vine-staff – a stick made from the wood of a plant which produces grapes

visor – a helmet's front part, which can be moved to cover the face

wattle and daub – twigs woven together with mud and straw

Index

aerial photographs 7
Aidan, Saint 65
Alban, Saint 51
Alfred, King 78–81, 82
Ambrosius Aurelianus 60
Anglesey 24, 26
Anglo-Saxon Chronicle, The 82, 94
Arthur, King 4–5, 58–60
Ashdown, Battle of 80
Athelney, Isle of 80
Augustine, Saint 66, 92
auxiliaries, Roman 22

ballista 28
Bath 44, 46–47
baths, Roman 16, 46–47
Bede 67, 76, 94
Beowulf 60–61, 70–71, 94
Boudica 26–27, 50
Britannia 91
Byrhtnoth 86–87

Caesar, Julius 18–19, 91, 94
cavalry, Roman 19, 22, 24
Celts 12–13
centurions 22
cevinus 31
chariot races 16, 49
Chedworth villa 38
Christianity 50, 64–67, 92
Christmas 64
Claudius, Emperor 19, 24, 50
Cnut, King 88–89
Colchester 26, 32, 34, 50
Colosseum 48
Columba 65
Constantine 53

Danelaw 80, 88
danegeld 88
days of the week 91
doctors 44–45
Dover 18
Druids 24–25
Durotriges 18, 19

Easter 92
Edington, Battle of 80
Edward the Confessor, King 89, 90, 92
Ethelbert, King 66, 72
Ethelred, King 88–89

farming 8, 12, 14, 56–57
Fishbourne Palace 38
forum 34, 36
Forum (Rome) 16
funerals, Roman 50
fyrd 81

Gaul 18, 32, 53, 70
gladiators 16, 44, 48
Glastonbury 59–60
gods, Anglo-Saxon 64, 91
gods, Roman 50
Gregory, Pope 66
Grime's Graves 8–9
groma 30
Guinevere 58–60

Hadrian's Wall 28–29, 44, 52
halls, Saxon 62
Hengist 55
hill forts 20
Honorius, Emperor 53
Horsa 55
hypocaust 38–39

Iceni tribe 26–27
Iona 65
Iron Age 12–15, 16, 24

Jarrow monastery 67, 76

Latin 42
legionaries, Roman 22, 28–29, 31
legions, Roman 18–19, 26–27, 28
Lindisfarne 65, 76
London 26

Maiden Castle 20–21
Maldon, Battle of 86–87
marriage 72–73
medicine 44–45, 73
Mithras 50
monasteries 65, 76
monks 65, 67, 82–83
months of the year 90, 91
mosaics 38, 51
Mount Badon, Battle of 60

ordeals 74
Oswald, King 65
Oswy, King 66

pastimes 84–85
Patrick, Saint 65
Picts 28, 52, 55
place-names: Roman 90
                    Saxon 57
                    Viking 80
punishments 49, 74–75

quern 14–15

radiocarbon dating 6–7
Redwald, King 70
roads 30–31, 90
Rockbourne villa 45
Rome 16–17, 48, 53
runic alphabet 83

sacrifices 24, 25, 46, 50, 51
sagas 84
St Albans 32
Saxon kingdoms 56
schools 42–43, 82
Scots 52
shops 36–37
Silchester 33, 34
Skara Brae 9
slaves 17, 40–41
sports 48–49, 84–85
standard-bearers, Roman 18, 23
stirrup 22, 91
Stone Age 8–9
Stonehenge 10–11, 25
Suetonius 26–27
Sutton Hoo 68–71

trepanning 45

Vespasian, General 20–21
villas 38–39, 53
Vortigern, King 55

wattle and daub 12, 56
wergilds 74–75
Wessex 56, 77, 78, 79, 80–81
Westminster Abbey 92
William, Duke of Normandy 89
Winchester 59, 78, 89
Witan 74
writing 42, 43, 83

York 28, 44
Yule 64